T0074638

Data Analytics in Marketing, Entrepreneurship, and Innovation

Data Analytics Applications

Series Editor:
Jay Liebowitz

Big Data in the Arts and Humanities
Theory and Practice
by Giovanni Schiuma and Daniela Carlucci
ISBN 978-1-4987-6585-5

Data Analytics Applications in Education
by Jan Vanthienen and Kristoff De Witte
ISBN: 978-1-4987-6927-3

Data Analytics Applications in Latin America and Emerging Economies
by Eduardo Rodriguez
ISBN: 978-1-4987-6276-2

Data Analytics for Smart Cities
by Amir Alavi and William G. Buttlar
ISBN 978-1-138-30877-0

Data-Driven Law
Data Analytics and the New Legal Services
by Edward J. Walters
ISBN 978-1-4987-6665-4

Intuition, Trust, and Analytics
by Jay Liebowitz, Joanna Paliszkiewicz, and Jerzy Gołuchowski
ISBN: 978-1-138-71912-5

Research Analytics
Boosting University Productivity and Competitiveness through Scientometrics
by Francisco J. Cantú-Ortiz
ISBN: 978-1-4987-6126-0

Sport Business Analytics
Using Data to Increase Revenue and Improve Operational Efficiency
by C. Keith Harrison and Scott Bukstein
ISBN: 978-1-4987-8542-6

Data Analytics and AI
by Jay Liebowitz
ISBN: 978-0-3678-9561-7

Data Analytics in Marketing, Entrepreneurship, and Innovation

Edited by
Mounir Kehal and Shahira El Alfy

CRC Press
Taylor & Francis Group
Boca Raton London New York

CRC Press is an imprint of the
Taylor & Francis Group, an **informa** business
AN AUERBACH BOOK

First edition published 2021
by CRC Press

6000 Broken Sound Parkway NW, Suite 300, Boca Raton, FL 33487-2742
and by CRC Press

2 Park Square, Milton Park, Abingdon, Oxon, OX14 4RN

ISBN 13: 978-0-367-69764-8 (pbk)
ISBN 13: 978-0-367-18483-4 (hbk)
ISBN 13: 978-0-429-19661-4 (ebk)

Typeset in Garamond
by codeMantra

Contents

Editors

Dr. Mounir Kehal is a professor in Business Analytics at Higher Colleges of Technology, Dubai, UAE. He gained a BSc in Computing and an MBA from the American International University in London, UK, an MPhil and PhD in Computing from the University of Surrey, Guildford, UK. He currently professes about analytics at Higher Colleges of Technology and applied research coordinator for HCT Dubai Campuses. Prior to which he was associate professor in Management Information Systems (MIS) (and was Dean) in the College of Business Administration at American University in the Emirates, Dubai, UAE. For many years, he was associate professor of Business Information Systems and director of Strategic Planning and Accreditations at École Supérieure de Commerce – Rennes School of Business, France. Prior to which, he was at the International University of Monaco – IUM, as assistant professor of Computing Science, Information Technology, Decision Systems and Knowledge Management. His area of research interest includes MIS, strategy, and education.

Dr. Shahira El Alfy is currently an assistant professor at Higher Colleges of Technology (HCT) in UAE. She holds a Doctorate in Business Administration—Marketing – and a Doctorate of Philosophy in Education Leadership. Dr. El Alfy's publications, conference papers, and research interests are in marketing of higher education, service management, and learning analytics.

Prior to joining HCT, Dr. El Alfy has been an assistant professor of marketing in the School of Business Administration at Ahram Canadian University (ACU). Dr. El Alfy has taught a wide range of courses at the undergraduate and postgraduate levels, including strategic marketing management, services marketing, integrated marketing communications, consumer behavior, international business, organization behavior, among other courses. Having an extensive teaching experience has enabled Dr. El Alfy to become an adjunct professor for postgraduates at the German University in Cairo (GUC), Eslsca Business School, and Arab Academy for Science and Technology. She has also supervised master's thesis of postgraduate students.

Over ten years of extensive industry experience in banking and corporate training has enhanced the contribution of Dr. El Alfy as an educator, mentor, and researcher.

Prior to her professional and academic career, Dr. El Alfy had an athletic career as an African table tennis champion who qualified and participated in 2000 Olympic Games in Sydney, Australia.

Contributors

Alia Al Jammal
Data Analyst
Dubai, United Arab Emirates

Mounir Kehal
Higher Colleges of Technology
Dubai Campuses
Dubai, United Arab Emirates

Pedro Longart
Business Division
Higher Colleges of Technology, Al Ain
Dubai, United Arab Emirates

Kennedy Prince Modugu
Business Division
Higher Colleges of Technology, Al Ain
Dubai, United Arab Emirates

Gerry N. Muuka
Department of Business Strategy,
    College of Business
Al Ghurair University
Dubai, United Arab Emirates

Sihle Ndlovu
Higher Colleges of Technology
Al Ruwais Women's Campus
Dubai, United Arab Emirates

Tabani Ndlovu
Higher Colleges of Technology
Madinat Zayed Women's Campus
Dubai, United Arab Emirates

Sujni Paul
Computer Information Science
Higher Colleges of Technology
Dubai, United Arab Emirates

Rajasekhara Mouly Potluri
Department of Marketing and
    International Business, College of
    Business
Al Ghurair University
Dubai, United Arab Emirates

Dustin White
Department of Economics
University of Nebraska at Omaha
    Omaha, Nebraska, USA

Lawal O. Yesufu
Department of Business Analytics,
    Faculty of Business
Higher Colleges of Technology
Sharjah, United Arab Emirates

Eman Zabalawi
Business Department
Higher Colleges of Technology
Dubai, United Arab Emirates

Chapter 1

Business Analytics: Through SIoT and SIoV

Mounir Kehal
Higher Colleges of Technology

Contents

Introduction

The Internet of Things (IoT) paradigm aims to lead us to a new era of computing where the Internet will expand to include billions of new types of devices. The IoT is based on the idea of integrating everyday smart objects equipped with sensors to the Internet. This way these heterogeneous objects become capable of communicating with each other and providing ubiquitous services, which opens a new vista of possibilities. All this pervasiveness will be enabled by sensors that range from battery-less radio frequency identification (RFID) to sensor devices equipped with many sensors. These devices sense different physical phenomena and can actuate different tasks. The cloud computing will provide the required infrastructure to gather and analyze the data generated by these sensors. This infrastructure will enable different applications by enabling the provision of end-to-end services. The analysis of this data will be important for businesses and governments, and eventually will become a key to create new business models.

The Social Internet of Things (SIoT) concept envisions enabling consciousness in the IoT by enabling social networking among the IoT devices (Atzori, Iera, Morabito, & Nitti, 2012). These devices will be able to socialize with each other and create social circles based on mutual interests and goals. This application of social networking will reuse the existing social network models and will address the IoT-specific issues such as scalability. Furthermore, the IoT devices will build trust-based relationships and will leverage these relationships for service provisioning. SIoT will enable the feasibility of managing the ever-growing number of devices in IoT.

Internet of Vehicles (IoV) is an emerging concept derived from its parent domain, IoT. The idea of IoV refers to the dynamic mobile communication between vehicles, infrastructure, drivers, and passengers. This communication is subdivided into V2V (vehicle to vehicle) when vehicles communicate with each other, V2I (vehicle to infrastructure) when vehicles communicate with RSUs (Road-Side Units) and V2H (vehicle to human) when vehicles communicate with drivers or the passengers of the vehicles. The key advantage of IoV is information sharing between different entities that can greatly benefit in improving the traffic on road. IoV promises great commercial interest and wide horizon for research that attracts a lot of researchers and companies (Maglaras, Al-Bayatti, He, Wagner, & Janicke, 2016). All time-connected environment for vehicles on roads provides enormous opportunities for governmental and nongovernmental organizations to connect with the drivers on the roads. For example, Traffic Regulatory Authorities can inform drivers to take an alternate route if there is an accident on the road ahead or if a construction work is in progress. This information can be directly integrated into vehicle navigation systems and effortlessly communicated through the Internet. This method of communicating with cars and drivers can significantly reduce the cost and effort by removing the expensive billboards on the roads.

Social Internet of Vehicles (SIoV) is the latest development in the area of IoV. It's following the trend of its sister concept, SIoT (Nitti, Girau, Floris, & Atzori, 2014). A key factor that makes SIoV exciting is the fact that vehicles can socialize with themselves and share information of common interests, e.g., road situations, nearby gas stations, and hotels. Socializing in SIoV is not limited to vehicles only as the network can include drivers, passengers, and infrastructure as well.

The main objective of this chapter is to discuss the perspective toward the utilizations and limitations of SIoV. Adaptability of latest technologies in countries makes them an excellent choice for utilizing SIoV and its applications. However, SIoV is still in its early ages and hence requires comprehensive research for development and deployment of these applications. This chapter will provide an insight into challenges and limitations anticipated in providing SIoV solutions.

The rest of this chapter is organized as follows: the Background section provides the introduction of SIoV through the review of literature. The main focus of this section presents the issues and challenges involved in designing and implementing SIoV applications. "Solutions and Recommendations" section delivers an insight into the proposed solutions to the challenges. "Future Research Directions" section provides the research directions in this field, and finally, the "Conclusion" section concludes this chapter.

Background

SIoV is comprised of social characteristics, human behavior, and network of vehicles. SIoV is sometimes referred to as vehicular social networks (VSNs) that are assumed to be a group of vehicles and individuals having common interests. SIoV is considered an important concept as vehicles can share a lot like personal information (e.g., location, destination, pictures), traffic information (e.g., accidents, road works, traffic jams), and other common interest information (e.g., nearby hotels, restaurant discounts, free parking slots). Figure 1.1 further illustrates the typical SIoV model.

SIoV is a perpetuation of VANETs (vehicular ad hoc networks). VANETs have been around for a few decades now and gained considerable attention from researchers. VANETs are a network of vehicles that can communicate with each other, infrastructure, and drivers. One of the major differences between VANETs and SIoV is that in VANETs, vehicles are not directly connected to the Internet and require an infrastructure (RSU) for connection, whereas in SIoV, all vehicles and infrastructure have Internet connectivity. Figure 1.2 further illustrates the typical VANET model.

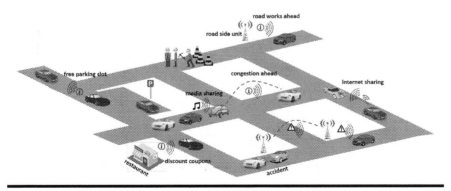

Figure 1.1   Typical model of Social Internet of Vehicles.

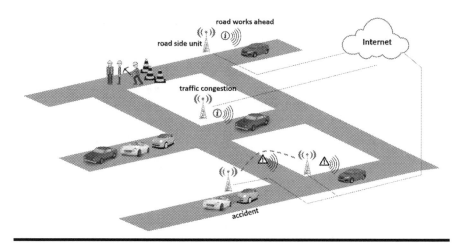

Figure 1.2 Typical model of Vehicular ad hoc networks.

SIoV is a fairly new concept in the field of Intelligent Transportation Systems (ITS) and mobile socializing, hence attracting researchers, academicians, and industry professionals. Several research projects are underway for development and deployment of SIoV applications. This section provides the review of literature to build a solid foundation for discussing the state-of-the-art applications along with their challenges and limitations for the region.

Lequerica, Longaron, and Ruiz (2010) discussed a mobile application Drive and Share (DaS), which is installed on passengers' mobile phones in the vehicle. The application assists passengers in sharing road information such as traffic and info-tainment based on their location using cellular network connection. Furthermore, the authors proposed an architecture that is expected to minimize the challenges of socializing in vehicular scenarios. The architecture is based on IP Multimedia Subsystems and the capabilities of vehicles to communicate with each other.

Bai and Krishnamachari (2010) presented a generic framework for enabling information-rich vehicular network applications for social, safety, and interactive services. They referred to this framework as IC NoW (Information Centric Networking on Wheels). The framework is proposed based on three key factors, namely, space, time, and user interest, and it ensures that protocols and applications are employed in a distributed manner based on decisions made locally. The framework is designed in a way that it can be easily integrated with currently available infrastructure of cellular providers. Furthermore, this framework enables modular design, facilitating easy application development, and creating a smooth migration path during the deployment of evolution path.

Smaldone, Han, Shankar, and Iftode (2008) proposed a framework for building communities on the road to facilitate the commuters. As a proof-of-concept, they presented a design of a VSN system they referred to as RoadSpeak that allows drivers to communicate with each other by joining different voice chat groups based on their location.

Maglaras et al. (2016) provide a comprehensive review of research and analysis of smart systems, including smart vehicles. The authors believe that with growth in the autonomous nature of the cars, several applications are being developed for both cars and passengers that can facilitate these entities by sharing information between them. This chapter provides a detailed overview of components and technologies involved in SIoV, context awareness, social network analysis methods, security and trust issues, and current challenges in drivers' privacy. The authors started by discussing the next generation of vehicles, including self-driving cars, electric cars, and the safety driving aspect of these future cars. Second, they highlighted the importance of enabling context awareness in vehicles while on road. The authors defined context awareness as the ability of the vehicles to adapt to the current contextual environment and provided three subsystems for it: sensing, reasoning, and acting. Sensing helps in gathering information through sensors depending upon the environment, e.g., location of the vehicle; reasoning processes the collected information and extracts high-level contextual data, e.g., detecting driver's fatigue level; and finally, acting facilitates in taking required action based on the data congregated, e.g., providing warning messages.

Furthermore, social network analysis in SIoVs is provided by discussing the centrality of entities in SIoVs. Centrality of the entities is helpful as it provides a metric of finding entities that are central to a group of vehicles and can act as a relay node to ensure efficient information dissemination. Another important concept besides centrality is clustering or grouping of vehicles based on varying parameters like speed, location, distance, and interests of the vehicles. This clustering of vehicles helps in avoiding broadcast storming (message duplication) problems, increasing throughput, and improving bit error rate.

Finally, the authors have discussed the security and privacy issues by highlighting different potential attacks such as denial of service, false message injection, masquerading, and impersonation attacks.

SIoV relations and interactions can be very complicated as they yield low-level details from the sensors and processing of this information is done at various layers before it can be delivered to the application layer. SIoV life cycle starts at the manufacturing site for the vehicles, where each vehicle is equipped with OBU (On-Board Unit) that forms a POR (Parental Object Relationship) with the manufacturer of the vehicle (Alam, Saini, & El Saddik, 2015). This relationship helps in providing information such as repairs, maintenance, and oil change. Another relationship of the vehicle is with HBU (Home Base Unit) through OBU that assists in connecting the vehicle to the owner's home, e.g., opening and closing of the garage gate. OBUs installed in vehicles can connect with RSUs to gather information like traffic congestion, alternate routes, free parking slots, and road closures. Finally, OBUs communicate with OBUs of the vehicles in vicinity that helps them socialize with their peer vehicles without interference from any other unit.

It makes profound sense for vehicles to create a network while traveling through highways as the communication time, destinations, speed, and topology are expected to be unchanged. Drivers of the vehicles can maintain a social profile like Facebook where they can share information and content like photos and videos while traveling. Individual drivers in this way can socialize with each other while driving on the highways that not only helps in keeping them up to date about the road conditions but also by making new contacts. Socializing on highways faces several challenges; however, two major challenges are vehicle high mobility and foreignness. To address these issues, Luan, Shen, and Bai (2015) provide a Social on Road (SOR) model. To tackle the issue of high vehicle mobility, SOR provides a proactive technique of estimating connection time between peer vehicles and stipulates peers that are expected to communicate for longer time based on their destinations. To solve the problem of foreignness, SOR provides a safe solution to guard sensitive user information during social communications.

Literature delivers a solid knowledge and understanding of current state of the art in the field of SIoV throughout the world by presenting the challenges and limitations identified by researchers along with the proposed solutions to these challenges. SIoV is currently in its early ages of development and hence requires extensive exploration that unleashes a wide spectrum of opportunities for manufacturers, vendors, developers, and governmental bodies. Developing countries are keen in deploying SIoV applications to automate safety on road.

The following section will provide a discussion of available applications of SIoV, their benefits to the regulatory bodies along with the issues; challenges; and problems in utilizing, developing, and deploying of SIoV applications.

Benefits and Advantages

There has been a surge in the number of people living in the urban world. This trend will continue, and it is estimated that the urban population will increase to 6.3 billion by 2050. This surge will eventually increase the number of mega cities. Therefore, it's the right time to deploy smart city solutions to manage the ever-growing population in such cities. In a smart city, smart mobility makes top at the list of other smart solutions such as smart environment, smart healthcare, smart energy, and smart industry. The main goal of smart mobility is to ensure intelligent and safe transport by utilizing IoV paradigm.

The IoV paradigm relies on both direct and indirect perception of vehicles to gather real-time information. The direct perception is based on the on-board sensor system that includes perceiving the vehicle, the driver and outside environment by using GPS, mileage recorder, and other sensors in the vehicle. However, indirect perception depends on the vehicle's communication with other vehicles, mostly within the same context. The data generated by both direct and indirect perception are communicated by either VANET or mobile (3G/4G) networks and are essential to enable the existing and novel applications.

The SIoV focuses on enabling the social relationships among vehicles that offer multifaceted benefits to the governments and their citizens. These relationships are established based on the contexts that include location, owner's profile, and mutual interests (Alam et al., 2015). The governments can provide unique services to their people by leveraging these social relationships. These services can fulfill requirements of various applications by delivering useful information (Kaiwartya et al., 2016). The ITS of a smart city can be enhanced with the SIoV to ensure ubiquitous connectivity of vehicles to collect real-time data and then to manage these data after applying intelligent analytics. The SIoV-enabled ITS system then works as a central hub where all data is collected and processed. This way the SIoV paradigm also enables governments to have more control in a smart city. This section explains the applications of SIoV with the focus on benefits offered to both government and citizens.

Safety Management

Ensuring traffic safety is the key goal of any ITS. The first category of safety applications utilizes sensors' data to improve the driver's performance. This is achieved by analyzing real-time sensed data to actuate automatic functions, such as wheel control, to enhance the quality of driving. Other applications rely on analytics of the real-time information shared between different vehicles. The SIoV guides different vehicles to decide what information needs to be shared with whom depending on the social relationships. This category of applications aid functions such as steering and speed control.

Another safety aspect is to monitor the overall condition of a vehicle and notify the driver and/or mechanic to book an appointment for repair. This diagnostic application depends on analytics of the vehicle sensor data sent to the cloud. The cloud applies analytics and predicts when the vehicle will require a repair. If a vehicle is parked at home, then the diagnostic application can use the configurations to automatically book an appointment with the driver's personal mechanic or otherwise can recommend the nearest or recommended service stations by using the social relationships with other vehicles. This application reduces the maintenance cost and avoids any technical faults that could lead to accidents.

In critical situations, these applications are beneficial to ensure safety in densely populated urban areas and highways. Furthermore, these applications trigger special calls in case of an emergency. These calls act like a black-box of the vehicle by providing context information such as location, number of passengers, and other details regarding the cause of the emergency. This shared data is used to warn other vehicles about the hazard on the road to avoid any further accidents.

Traffic Control and Convenience

The SIoV enables many useful applications for the convenience of vehicles, and better traffic management applications are dependent on social relationships based on current location information provided by the GPS. This information is essential for real-time traffic control application that is used in ITS to avoid congestions by effectively managing the traffic (Wan, Liu, Shao, Vasilakos, Imran, & Zhou, 2016). The location data is communicated in real time by vehicles using heterogeneous networks to the centralized or decentralized cloud. The ITS update other vehicles about the congested areas and suggest alternative routes. The electronic toll system uses the RFID chip information to ensure the smooth flow of traffic.

Convenient parking applications guide drivers to find the nearest empty parking spaces. These applications rely on accurate location information of the parked vehicles who have some kind of or a social relationship based on being parked in same parking areas, for instance. The benefits of utilizing these applications include reduction in time required for parking that eventually leads to low carbon emission. Another important category of applications tailors the routes for users by using their profiles. These applications aim to optimize the resources such as fuel, comfort, and money, by using multiple modes of transportation in the recommended routes. These multimode routes ensure to reduce the congestion and carbon emission in densely populated urban areas.

Some social relationship-based applications could help a driver to fix any hardware- or software-based issues by connecting him to someone from his social circle who can guide him using text, audio, or video chat. In case of no suitable match, the application can utilize cloud-based services to provide a related guidance tutorial. These applications aim to bring down the repairing and maintenance costs. Moreover, remote telematics applications allow drivers to remotely control their vehicles by replacing the traditional physical interaction-based operations. These applications use secure methods to ease the monitoring of vehicles and other operations such as remote locking a car.

Productivity

The SIoV-based relationships can be exploited by novel applications to reduce the traffic and allow infotainment between vehicles. This can be achieved by creating social groups of cars, the owners of which are willing to share their cars with potential car service seekers. Both owners allow their vehicles to join such groups where seekers are sharing their profile and requirements for car sharing. The owners' configurations are matched to seekers' profiles, and allocation is done between optimal candidates. The matching criteria could include information such as pickup and destination address, age, gender, and job designation. However, this type of service demands strict verification of seekers and car owners to ensure safety for both driver and passengers. Moreover, some infotainment applications allow vehicles to share their connectivity with other cars in their social circle using Wi-Fi Direct technology.

Commercialization

Insurance industry and other businesses can be benefited by using the data generated by vehicles and social relationships between them. The SIoV allows vehicles to join premier groups of safe driving practitioners based on the analytics of their recorded data. These data consist of months of data records to give insights on the driving behavior and the statistics of traffic rules violations during trips in different areas. Insurance companies can reward these elite groups of vehicles by cutting their insurance cost. Other businesses can also buy their subscription to target their potential customers traveling in vehicles using tailored advertisements depending on the shared user information and other spatial or temporal context information. These applications rely on smart cloud-based services.

Issues, Controversies, Problems

The SIoV aims to integrate multiple vehicles and users using heterogeneous network technologies. The benefits of SIoV will enable the provision of services to a plethora of applications to provide a more reliable, efficient, and manageable system. This section describes the issues that are instrumental in putting the limit to the adaptation rate of the SIoV.

1. *Standardization*:

   One of the key issues in developing and implementing SIoV architecture and applications is the lack of standardization at variable degrees in diverse contexts. Currently, no standards are available to tackle issues like interoperability, types of hardware and software, use of frequencies, protocols, and communication technology. SIoV is expected to be influenced by different entities like governmental organizations for devising laws and policies, manufacturers of the vehicles for manufacturing smart vehicles that can socialize, and third-party vehicle spare parts vendors for installing additional components like navigation systems and sensors. Presently, no standard rule or policy is available for any of the above-mentioned entities. For example, no standard policy from governmental law enforcing agencies is available that can serve as a guideline for vehicles on how to socialize on roads. Similarly, no governmental rule is available regarding the use of communication technology on roads for vehicles. Furthermore, due to the lack of policies, there is a gap between different vehicle manufacturers and different third-party vendors to unite at mutual parameters, e.g., use of communication technologies, protocols, hardware, and software. Due to this lack of unity, different vendors and manufacturers are delivering vehicles and their components at their own standards, hence creating difficulty in communication between vehicles and ultimately socialization of vehicles.

2. *Adaptability*:

   Embracing innovative technologies by people has always been an issue throughout the world. Many countries have the same issues when it comes to accepting new technologies. SIoV is an emerging concept which is currently lacking in applications; however, it has great potential for developing and implementing applications that can ease daily life operations. A major feature of SIoV is socializing and sharing of information; however, information sharing might not appeal to a lot of users in some countries because of several factors such as culture, privacy, trust, security, anonymity, and automation. Due to these issues, many people might not feel very comfortable in adapting to SIoV.

3. *Scalability*:

Provision of better quality of experience is vital to the wide acceptance of SIoV internationally. The performance of SIoV is limited by the scalability of the infrastructure to handle dynamic rates of traffic in different areas. The traffic rates vary a lot; the traffic surges during the peak periods of a day and on special events. Moreover, the shape of the SIoT structure could add in to scalability issue by increasing the time for service provisioning in a dynamic vehicle network. The required quality of service for SIoV to provide better quality of experience is limited by the scalability issues that should be solved to attract the masses.

4. *Infrastructure*:

Many countries are developing at a rapid pace; however, they are still lacking in infrastructure when it comes to latest technological concepts like SIoV. ITS have started appearing in many countries, e.g., toll collection using RFID. Although many countries are supporting new concepts like ITS, still, SIoV might require more infrastructure than currently deployed, e.g., RSUs, parking sensors, and OBUs. Development and deployment of these infrastructures require high cost, which might be one of the major issues in pursuing toward adoption of SIoV by some countries at governmental level. Furthermore, as discussed earlier, currently, no standard policies are in place in some countries for developing and deploying infrastructure for SIoV; hence, infrastructure vendors have no solid path for creating devices for SIoV for implementation in some countries.

5. *Lack of applications*:

The novel infotainment and user convenience applications are required to attract more users to actively engage in SIoV paradigm for its success. There are several applications of SIoV as was aforementioned. However, these applications only exist in theory and lack the novel infotainment third-party applications. The big mobile software provider companies, Apple and Google, have introduced CarPlay and Android Auto to compete for the in-car applications (Massaro et al., 2017). Governments will need to make sure that new business models are created of SIoV paradigm based on novel applications.

6. *Security*:

The security of individual vehicles is critical in the context of SIoV. The consequence of comprising the security of even a single vehicle could be disastrous for the other vehicles in the context and even risk the reliable functioning of other components in the ITS infrastructure. The security issue is more challenging in SIoV domain that is enabled by heterogeneous and distributed technologies (Zheng, Zheng, Chatzimisios, Xiang, & Zhou, 2015). Furthermore, the connectivity between the location-based groups makes the security issue more complicated to address because of the several different locations, heterogeneous manufacturers, and owners of vehicles. The security needs to be foolproof at all links, including communication between vehicles, between vehicles to infrastructure, between infrastructure to cloud, and between the cloud and applications. Therefore, the SIoV will be prone to different security threats, and to successfully avoid these threats is still an open research challenge. The security risk of getting unreliable information that can result in hazardous situations poses a hurdle in the acceptance of SIoV.

7. *Privacy*:

The privacy of user information is extremely important to be ensured to encourage the users to adopt to new technologies (Derikx, de Reuver, & Kroesen, 2016). It is vital to ensure privacy because of the relatively conservative culture in most of the countries. In SIoV, the data is shared between different vehicles and analyzed by cloud to offer different services. The privacy becomes an issue because of the security risks at different stages of the SIoV. Moreover, the social groups can introduce other privacy issues such as identity theft. Therefore, the SIoV should follow the principles of privacy by design to satisfy the privacy requirements to ensure privacy such as anonymity and not being linkable. Data should normally be anonymized in such a way that the real identities of the users are not revealed even if the data is leaked from the system. After anonymity, the other aspect is that the attacker will be unable to link different data items to a single user. Moreover, governments need to come up with policies to enable transparency so that the people can trust the system rather than being paranoid by themselves.

Information Management in SIoVs

Information management entails knowledge and various methods for communication, storage, interaction, data gathering, authentication, validation, data distribution, and fault tolerance. In SIoVs, information can be categorized into safety and non-safety information, for instance. Information based on the safety of drivers, passengers, and vehicles is essential in applications contributing toward providing ITS services like congestion information, accident warnings, alternate routes, traffic signals, dangerous curves, weather conditions, speed information, toll gates, and infotainment such as sharing of media and hotspots. SIoV is vastly dependent on the information from various sources and requires processing of data to avoid information duplication, unreliability in data delivery, and delay. Furthermore, information is expected to be secure from various attacks, should be coming from trustworthy sources, data delivery should be based on real time, and privacy concerns should be properly addressed.

The security of the transportation network is a dynamic aspect of SIoVs, as the compromise of a vehicle can lead to life-threatening situations, as well as a general degradation of other components that use the SIoV as part of a city infrastructure. Hence, some major security threats for SIoVs could be resolved by the potential solutions that a respective information system ought to provide, e.g., issues in relation to:

- *Malware*: such as viruses or worms, is usually introduced through outside unit software and firmware updates, for example. Malware can infect vehicles and even allow remote adversaries to take control of individual vehicles. Remote access Trojans, paired with the advanced communication facilities that SIoVs may have, can gain control of the system and thus interrupt vital services.
- *Masquerading (or Camouflage Attack)*: Through such an attack, a vehicle fakes its credentials and pretends to be legitimate in the network. Interlopers may conduct attacks, such as injecting false messages or having multiple identities to be multiple legitimate vehicles concurrently. They can disorder traffic and affect other drivers through the steering systems.
- *Distributed Denial of Service (DDOS)*: Such attacks aim to prevent genuine users from accessing data or services in computer networks. In vehicular networks, this attack would flood and may gridlock the traffic with large volumes of extraneous messages that would negatively impact the communication between the network's nodes, OBUs and RSUs. Because the vehicle under attack is part of the wider infrastructure of the SIoV, there would be high-powered computing infrastructure near the targeted component.

Solutions and Recommendations

There is a great scope and benefits of SIoV. However, there are undoubtedly various issues that need to be addressed for the successful deployment and adoption of SIoV. This section covers the details of such solutions and recommendations for successful deployment and adaptation of SIoV.

Governments will have to work closely with vendors and manufacturers to encourage the research and innovation in SIoV. These governments need to establish cross-industrial cooperation to reap the benefits of SIoV. Governments will need to form a consortium to agree on the employment of different technologies and data-sharing standards. Moreover, these countries will have to come up with mutual policies for SIoV.

The focus of countries should be to take initiatives in promoting the SIoV applications to increase awareness of its adaptation in different sectors such as automobiles and insurance. These efforts should comply with the ultimate public demand of having convenient, safe, and cost-saving means of travel. Furthermore, the governments should explore and fund the SIoV applications to be used in disaster management. Similarly, these governments need to agree on policies and laws to address data privacy issues.

The whole process of deployment of SIoV system should be conducted in multiple stages. The early deployment stages can offer simple features to act like a test-bed environment. The systems need to be checked against different threats in the environments before they are made available to general public to improve the security. These early deployments can be based on basic vehicle communication to enable applications based on only critical data sharing between vehicles. The lessons learned from these deployments will provide a feedback loop for next stages to reduce the risk. This gradual deployment process will not only improve based on the users' feedback, but also give time for adaptation.

Future Research Directions

To appreciate SIoVs, we need to study major topical issues such as data redundancy, scalability, and synchronization. Thorough specification portrayal of SIoV is important to comprehend the impact of payload on VANET's infrastructure. A specialist domain ontology tailored to support the SIoV can be an important part of future work to inject intelligence and terminology-driven communication in the virtual entities. Strategies to leverage the smart connections in cyber-physical SIoV is also a viable future work. Additionally, practical deployment of a system and using it to collect real-life IoV-related multimodal sensory data in city or urban areas can be another interesting direction.

There are different measures that can be taken to deal with the data redundancy, scalability, and synchronization issues in a highly dynamic SIoV. The decentralized cloud-based architecture (Fog computing) (Gerla, Lee, Pau, & Lee, 2014) should be considered. This decentralized architecture will be helpful to improve the quality of experience for the SIoV users. Also, the SIoV social structure should be shaped to make the discovery and provisioning of services more efficient.

Conclusion

This chapter presents the evolution of VANET to SIoV and highlights the range of new services that can be enabled by this domain. Furthermore, it discusses different research efforts and applications that are being coined by the research community. It also focuses on the benefits and advantages of SIoV by discussing the impact of this new paradigm to novel applications to increase productivity and efficiency, while introducing new business models. It is also emphasized that the SIoV is a new domain, and it has a range of technical as well as social issues that are pertinent to societal dynamics and government policies. The role of information management will be key to managing privacy while taking advantage of the SIoV potential. This chapter recommends various solutions and identifies the future research directions to deal with the inherent issues of SIoV. The cooperative efforts of governments to mutually design and implement policies for SIoV and then iteratively deploy its infrastructure by reflecting on the feedback are the key requirements for the successful adoption of this contemporary technology.

References

Alam, K. M., Saini, M., & El Saddik, A. (2015). Toward social internet of vehicles: Concept, architecture, and applications. *IEEE Access*, 3, 343–357.

Atzori, L., Iera, A., Morabito, G., & Nitti, M. (2012). The social internet of things (siot)– when social networks meet the internet of things: Concept, architecture and network characterization. *Computer Networks*, 56(16), 3594–3608.

Bai, F., & Krishnamachari, B. (2010). Exploiting the wisdom of the crowd: Localized, distributed information-centric VANETs [Topics in Automotive Networking]. *IEEE Communications Magazine*, 48(5), 138–146.

Derikx, S., de Reuver, M., & Kroesen, M. (2016). Can privacy concerns for insurance of connected cars be compensated? *Electronic Markets*, 26(1), 73–81.

Gerla, M., Lee, E. K., Pau, G., & Lee, U. (2014, March). Internet of vehicles: From intelligent grid to autonomous cars and vehicular clouds. In *2014 IEEE World Forum on Internet of Things (WF-IoT)* (pp. 241–246). IEEE.

Kaiwartya, O., Abdullah, A. H., Cao, Y., Altameem, A., Prasad, M., Lin, C. T., & Liu, X. (2016). Internet of vehicles: Motivation, layered architecture, network model, challenges, and future aspects. *IEEE Access*, 4, 5356–5373.

Lequerica, I., Longaron, M. G., & Ruiz, P. M. (2010). Drive and share: Efficient provisioning of social networks in vehicular scenarios. *IEEE Communications Magazine*, 48(11), 90–97.

Luan, T. H., Lu, R., Shen, X., & Bai, F. (2015). Social on the road: Enabling secure and efficient social networking on highways. *IEEE Wireless Communications*, 22(1), 44–51.

Maglaras, L. A., Al-Bayatti, A. H., He, Y., Wagner, I., & Janicke, H. (2016). Social internet of vehicles for smart cities. *Journal of Sensor and Actuator Networks*, 5(1), 3.

Massaro, E., Ahn, C., Ratti, C., Santi, P., Stahlmann, R., Lamprecht, A., ... Huber, M. (2017). The car as an ambient sensing platform [Point of view]. *Proceedings of the IEEE*, 105(1), 3–7.

Nitti, M., Girau, R., Floris, A., & Atzori, L. (2014, May). On adding the social dimension to the internet of vehicles: Friendship and middleware. In *2014 IEEE International Black Sea Conference on Communications and Networking (BlackSeaCom)* (pp. 134–138). IEEE.

Smaldone, S., Han, L., Shankar, P., & Iftode, L. (2008, April). Roadspeak: Enabling voice chat on roadways using vehicular social networks. In *Proceedings of the 1st Workshop on Social Network Systems* (pp. 43–48). ACM.

Wan, J., Liu, J., Shao, Z., Vasilakos, A. V., Imran, M., & Zhou, K. (2016). Mobile crowd sensing for traffic prediction in internet of vehicles. *Sensors*, 16(1), 88.

Zheng, K., Zheng, Q., Chatzimisios, P., Xiang, W., & Zhou, Y. (2015). Heterogeneous vehicular networking: A survey on architecture, challenges, and solutions. IEEE Communications Surveys & Tutorials, 17(4), 2377–2396.

Chapter 2

Innovation Analytics

Eman Zabalawi
Higher Colleges of Technology

Alia Al Jammal
Project Management Institute

Contents

Introduction

The scope of innovation analytics and new product development (NPD) analytics has greatly expanded with the advent of "big data," which is a collection of structured and unstructured data from multiple sources inside and outside organizations. More data becomes available from external sources; big data and analytics is a crucial basis for business innovation and competitiveness. Analytics is an integral part of the innovation lifecycle by knowing the existing situation and foreseeing the future to make smarter decisions to optimize innovation and business performance for competitive advantage, synthesizing data from internal and external sources into insights, and actionable future events. Analytics provides the means to make faster and better fact-based decisions that respond to exceptions and issues within the internal and external environment. In analyses, every action becomes magnified at different managerial levels. Predictive and prescriptive analytics proves extremely valuable in the tiers of organizations to higher management, where lower-level managers concerned with day-to-day operations will likely have no use for statistical modeling and be better served using a platform specializing in descriptive and diagnostic capabilities. Whatever the requirements, it helps to know the lay of the land, as well as a bit of the local parlance, to navigate the data analytics landscape.

Businesses' analytics environment is organized around processes; integration of people; and integration of knowledge, quality, and service (Juran, 1989; Johnson & Kaplan, 1987; Harrington, 1991; Hamel & Prahalad, 1994). In process management, the tasks are handed out in process-teams with a hands-on approach to the whole process, which yields to a recorded data, outcomes, and measures to success (Lewis, 1995; Hammer & Champy, 1993). It is a new paradigm treated as a strategic corporate priority due to the promising implementation of good knowledge-based practices by using business internal and external data as a journey of an analytical approach to doing business, improving business, and innovating business.

Scope of Innovation Analytics

Product innovation is the development of new products and improves existing products and services as a core to survival in the modern economy. Therefore, enhancing innovation abilities is currently the *driver* of corporate growth and prosperity. This chapter will focus on innovation analytics as a critical success factor for successful innovation. What analytics applies to product development? What analytics supports managers in making decisions? Moreover, how to diffuse innovative analytics at organizations? Developing products reflects the voice of the customer as a customer-focused strategy to new product process is critical to success. Doing the due diligence to data collection, data analysis, and data modeling is vital to success before product development pays off! Analytics is undergoing a revolution in the adoption of new products and services development for gaining a competitive advantage.

Innovation Theory is based on organizational vision and knowledge management, i.e., facilitating the development—integration and application of knowledge—based upon organizational vision, which is anticipated to give directions for knowledge management, which led to entrepreneurialism (Peters, 1987), accountability, agility, and the moving of decision-making closer to the customer and the removing of management layers (Schaaf, 1995; Prahald & Hamel, 1996). In this transition, the focus on knowledge as a productive resource for innovation, economic growth, and survival, in addition to the productivity of the knowledge workers, has received increasing attention during the 1990s. The persons who have discussed this theme extensively have been, among others, Toser (1990), Reich (1991), Quinn (1992), Drucker (1993), Archibugi and Michie (1995), Lundvall (1992), Lundvall and Johnson (1994), in addition to Nonaka and Takeuchi (1995) and Leonard-Barton (1995). Innovation in this context will be seen as the positioning of companies in a globalized knowledge-based economy (Freeman, 1995; Landabaso, 1995). In the new perspectives, it is in particular technological changes, integration, and practical application of knowledge, which are the focal elements to development (Grant, 1996; Fruin, 1997; Stewart, 1997; Sveiby, 1997).

Most employees of companies are highly qualified, educated professionals. Their work consists of converting information to knowledge, applying competencies in production of product or service, with the assistance of suppliers' knowledge. Certain firms have more information than others, and turning this into knowledge gives them an advantage in ascertaining market indecencies, putting their employees in a better position to innovate. This requires systematic efforts and a high degree of organization (Drucker, 1993, p. 173). Thus, as a source of competitive advantage, the value-added comes from the members of the organization called new growth theory (Scott, 1989); it is a center in the knowledge-based theory (Grant, 1996) by defining knowledge as systematizing and structuring information for a specific purpose (Johnnessen et al., 1997).

Systems Theory is a systemic knowledge that reflects how we know, i.e., the patterns that combine the experience of what happened (process) and the product, as a process explained by Maturana and Varela (1987, p. 24) of how we think along with what type of explicit knowledge is relevant and meaningful. In the digital data world, data analytics is the process, and data modeling is the competitive product position that supports organizational innovation and enables knowledge integration.

New Product Development that survives the screening stage of new product development (NPD) requires a more sophisticated and detailed business analysis to determine if a product are substantial users' needs. Product meaningfulness concerns the benefit that users receive from buying and using a new product, or new product outperforms (Rijsdijk, Langerak, and Jan, 2011). Note also that "product" means not only the evident or physical product but the "extended product"—the entire bundle of benefits associated with the product, including the system supporting the product, product service, and support, as well as the product's image. Therefore, during the innovation and NPD life cycle, the innovator will need to answer many different questions using multiple types of innovation analytics: first is descriptive analytics such as what happened and why did it happen that way? Reviewing the market, competitor research, and customers feedback determines the selling price of the product. Second is situational: what is happening now, and why is it happening?

Identify the product's market potential through the review of market research and the sales performance of existing products in the range. Use recent sales figures and industry sales figures to help identify the current level of market activity and interest in products in the same line as a new product. The third is predictive of what is likely to happen, and what should the innovator do about it? Forecast sales volume is to estimate the volume of the product sales anticipated based on customer needs, existing customer base, and market size. Fourth is prescriptive; if we do this, what is the best action to take? Fifth is evaluative—what are the risks of doing something, or not? Identify break-even point to estimate the profitability of the product, and determine break-even point—the amount of product that needs to be sold to cover fixed costs (such as rent, electricity, and wages). Determine the minimum sale price of the project returns based on anticipated discounted product prices to identify the lowest sales figure per item. Consider the long term by forecasting the lifespan of a product in the market. How long will it be relevant to the market's consumers? How long will it take to realize a decent return on investment? What market share percentage does it have the potential to realize? Business analysis eliminates inappropriate ideas and avoids unnecessary costs. The following steps are common to assess the viability of a new product or service.

The scope of the strategy is to determine how to position a new product in the marketplace and how to develop new products and services. The information gathered from the data analytics testing the market helps to identify which market to target and how. The use of data shapes business strategies by identifying relevant market and product information as well as approaches to development, and differentiation flow NPD employing process to link all variables. Managers require to develop a dynamic planning method that is innovative, efficient, and flexible for NPD in an analytics culture by combining analytics effectively in every role in a systematic approach illustrated in the following sections.

Managers and Analytics Applications

The amount of information available within the organization and the data from market study are becoming timely to use rather than an insight but to add value to the business and the economy assessing the impact of all business partners. Managers strive to know what happened and why it happened, which are no longer adequate; moreover, what is happening now, what is to happen next, and what actions could be taken are the optimal knowledge to add value and win the global market in a fast-changing industry due to the artificial intelligence (AI) influence.

Analytics is a differentiator, to turn challenges to opportunities depending on how organizations and managers transform data and its analytics and information. Three levels of analytics capability emerge at a managerial level: operational, experienced, and transformed; each has a distinct use of stages of analytics adoption. Aspirational is to achieve the desired outcome focusing on efficiency and existing process searching for ways to cut costs. Experienced analytics often goes beyond cost management by developing a better approach to collect, incorporate, and act on analytics effectively, so they can optimize and exceed goals.

The ability to use analytics as a competitive differentiation and adopted data analysis at the organization level among people, processes, and tools to optimize their differentiation with automating operations through effective use of data insights requires a transformed organization that has substantial experience using analytics across a broad range of functions. Aim to focus on driving customer profitability and making targeted investments in niche analytics. Transformed organizations grow three times more likely than aspirational organizations due to their aspiration of a higher level used of analytics adoptions.

The barriers that organizations face are managerial and cultural resistance to data analytics and the use of data rather than the data collection process and its accuracy. The leading obstacle in analytics adoption is a lack of understanding of how to use analytics to improve the business due to individual competencies. The information must become understood and acted upon as managers want a better way to communicate sophisticated insights to quickly absorb the meaning of the data and take action such as the emerging approach to reports formats and segregation of categories that makes information come alive, which includes data visualization and process simulation and other productive and prescriptive techniques that are user-friendly. New tools can make insights and access to data more accessible and fast to understand to act on its components transforming numbers into information, an insight that can be readily put to use instead of having to rely on further interpretation due to uncertainty about how to act. It takes strategic plans forward to gain the benefits of analytics with specific management approaches.

To successfully implement analytics-driven management to create value, as a new path to reduce time to value created by focusing on the most prominent and highest-value opportunities, by using data and its analytics and information outcome, the manager better insight the risks comes with it countering the prevailing strategic business direction. Within each opportunity, middle managers start with questions, form a problem statement to meet the business objective, and identify those pieces of data needed for solving the problem stated. Last, after defining the desired insight, it can target specific subject to available data to be analyzed to illuminate gaps in the data infrastructure and business processes, avoiding wasting time in cleaning up unwanted data in unmanageable sheets to take factual approach actions. Therefore, information found from an insight is tenfold in its ability to execute and boost business value with less operational challenges. To summarize, data, insights, and timely actions linked to the business purpose must always be in view. Data and its analysis get accepted, rejected, or improved based on business needs. The truth is that it is not enough to be "data-driven." Today's managers need to take care to prepare their data so that it reflects reality, understands what types of analysis to apply, derives meaningful conclusions, and communicates them effectively in terms of revenue growth and operating efficiency of an outperforming organization.

As analytics becomes central to decisions across finance, marketing, human resource, and operations related to work, it is also vital for continuous learning efforts within organizations. In the context of analytics-related continuous learning within different functions, managers need to differentiate among types of analytics applications used for function-specific decision-making. What are the current and future applications of different types of analytics? Types of analytics are descriptive, predictive, prescriptive, and big data analytics, which can help support different dimensions of managerial work planning, implementing, and controlling in four business functions. What are the current and future uses of various analytics applications? Will data analytics change the nature of the supply chain and require companies to add new services in order to stay relevant?

Types of data analytics are used as a process of extracting, transforming, loading, modeling, and drawing conclusions from data to make decisions. It is the "concluding" side of business intelligence tools with extracting, transforming, and loading steps at the database level. There are four ways of data once the data is formatted to a report form; these are descriptive, diagnostic, predictive, and prescriptive analytics.

Descriptive analytics is used to construct a narrative of the past, quantitatively describing the main features of a collection of data—the first step in a complicated process that provides a solid foundation for further analytics. It helps to envision a possible future and is designed to get necessary expository information: who, what, when, where, how many? It describes a set of data, such as informative sales linked to representatives' reports for sales quotas, while the use of predictive and prescriptive analytics is to envision future. Descriptive analytics is applied to large volumes of data, such as census data, for example, an insight into average sales volume daily/weekly/monthly. What descriptive analytics cannot explain is why an action happened and only what happened. It is used to provide powerful insights into simple arithmetic operations such as mean, median, mode, or minimum and maximum values. Current useful tools for descriptive analytics are Microsoft Excel, SPSS, and STATA.

Diagnostic analytics is used for the question of "why the action?"—queries to enable further requests to explain surprising values. Diagnostic analytics provides essential, actionable insights as it helps bring an understanding of causal relationships by looking backward in time. It can be on a larger scale from descriptive to diagnostic needs. For example, employee work hours might reveal the performance gap. Diagnostic analytics provides answers to questions such as "how effective was the promotion campaign based on customers' response in different regions in comparison with time factor?" Alternatively, "why has sales decreased/increased from last year?" The common techniques in diagnostic analytics are drill-down, correlations, probabilities, and identifying patterns.

Predictive analytics is used to identify what is likely to happen in the future after two previous quality findings analyzing the past; now its future such as trends in relationships between variables determines the strength of their correlation—also used to hypothesize causality. Statistical modeling and predictive modeling go hand in hand, for example, the use of statistical modeling to determine how closely revenue correlates with an area of population, gross income, and several homeowners. It is also used to predict revenue value for a region or new branch location. One known example of predictive analytics is demand forecasting, where organizations use historical data to predict, for example, what next month's demand is going to be. When such a model is accurate enough, decisions could be based on it to support maintaining lower levels of inventory or higher-order value. Examples of useful tools for predictive analytics are Python, MATLAB, and RapidMiner.

Prescriptive analytics is the last which answers the question of *which action to take* to gain a future advantage or mitigate a threat. Prescriptive analytics suggests all favorable outcomes and which courses of action need to be taken to reach a particular outcome. An example is an AI "what if" based on numerous variables with big data reflecting crowd behavior used to refine the AI's decisions over time capabilities. An example of prescriptive analytics is the recommendation of Netflix recommending similar shows to what was watched. Alternatively, the rating is used to recommend an item to another user who has a similar taste (Gartner, 2018).

Optimization of data analytics leads to understanding, interpreting, and leveraging data that drives these processes and experts facing enterprises and how to mitigate risks by data foresight to how we want the future to happen. Foresight and predictive analytics specialize in market intelligence, analytics, and forecasting. The aim is not to conduct "market research" but to forecast the future and put current plans to reach that optimal future by making the most accurate and well-grounded decision while taking into account all currently available information.

Diffusion of Innovation Analysis— Creating the Environment

Leaders do not just embrace analytics and actionable insights; they offer innovation of new developments that exceed the customers' needs. It is the data foresight of how the company wants the future to be by promoting excellent data quality and accessibility lab to build a qualitative and quantitative innovation culture by embedding innovation and analytics as part of every role. Moreover, decisions based on data-driven techniques and models for NPD were analytics information that is delivered in a variety of formats evident from departmental and individual dashboards by creating a variety of databases such as charts, spreadsheets, alerts via emails or text messages, audio complaint recordings, and many more.

Analytics could be challenging because the specialized nature of tools and approaches makes the business value less accessible to business users. Therefore, business analysis skills are required to design, deliver, and interpret data. Providing data analytics training in the increasing complexity of the technology and the increasing data sources with new approaches for leveraging data is crucial. Leaders need to equip employees with the analytics knowledge and skills to reap the innovative rewards of big data.

Business intelligence and analytics dashboards need to be open source for employees with friendly tools that are set up for analysis and decision-making of the most significant business need. Include analytics and innovation in every role. New opportunities will open up after the exploit of data and analytics technologies to improve and transform the businesses to innovate across all levels. Leaders analyze and interpret data to transform strategies into actionable insights and foresight to succeed from customer-generated data. Use big data more aggressively across all the organizations.

Enable more extensive use of big data and analytics. Managers leverage big data and analytics more effectively over a broader range of organizational processes and functions throughout the innovation process, from new ideas to creating new business models and developing new products and services.

Infuse analytical capabilities throughout the organization to spark innovation by focusing on end-user analytic tools. Embrace customer insight and opinion. Collect and analyze customer-generated data, and create customer interaction environments.

Build skills, cross-train, and co-locate analytics and innovation teams to create networks of trust and shared objectives, and cross-pollinate points of view and discoveries and share a common trait: the ability to employ data and analytics to support innovation successfully.

It is setting ethical standards for data scientists. It assures base-level data scientist competency supported with core values and policy of use. It includes trusted, structured sources for repeatable, relatively slow, and expensive descriptive reporting processes.

Set a data science lab, which caters to advanced predictive and prescriptive analytics that are often detailed, complex, and unique. The process can be somewhat slow and laborious, but can ultimately result in high-impact results.

Define a business challenge to solve. This can be *exploratory* (for example, determining what factors contribute to a consumer's default on a bank loan) or *predictive* (for example, predicting when the next natural gas leak will occur and what factors will drive the next failure). Start small and build in stages. Do not "boil the ocean" on your initial attempts. Evolve your approach over time.

Partner with the data science team. Work with this team to deliver a data and processing environment for the data needed to address the defined business challenge. Enable a platform that will scale to execute the required models and algorithms. This environment might be cloud-based.

Finally, data and analytics technical professionals must keep the end goal in mind. It is easy to become enamored of new technology choices, but the business value must be front and center in every decision. It is essential to maintain open channels of communication with constituents, both internal and external—and to explain any industrial actions or concepts that one can understand, support, and champion. This is an exciting time for data and analytics professionals, in which they can play an increasingly critical role in helping the organization achieve business.

The Cases of Transformation for the Digital Future

Netflix Innovation Analytics

Netflix is one of the leading digital streaming service providers within the entertainment industry, co-founded by Marc Randolph and Reed Hastings in 1997 (Netflix), who later forewent the DVD delivering service. This business first establishes the concept that innovations are not restricted in the format of a product but also as a service.

Second, the subscribing fee introduces the commercialization of Netflix's new approach in delivering entertainment. The traditional management textbook theories would have predicted that Netflix should have now failed, while it showed a successful growth in its business after starting the video streaming in 2007 and reaching 94 million members globally by the end of 2016. Their success was driven from its focus on the power of data and analytics, as an example, the development of Cinematch, which better predicts the pattern of the request of DVD titles by subscribers in addition to establishing an open competition (Netflix Prize) that enables anyone to win $1 million prizes for improving its algorithms. Netflix is a data-driven company before data and analytics drive the current market (Venkatraman, Explorer, 2016).

Netflix's innovation was focused on two dimensions: logistics and analytics; also, its digital business transformation appeared in technology and data and analytics. Through technology, Netflix worked with Amazon to develop a world-class back-end infrastructure. Through Amazon Web Services, Netflix could quickly deploy thousands of servers and terabytes of storage within a short time; it collected the most detailed data possible to be the best at knowing their customers on an individual basis. Everything that Netflix provides today to their customers is a recommendation. Based on its strategic relationship with Facebook, Netflix has been able to add more useful data to make its recommendation even more powerful. So, everything Netflix offers to an individual is personal but supported by compelling data and analytics. Netflix has been able to take its information advantage with big data and analytics to a further step, at capitalizing on technology developments and taking advantage of information-driven data to continually refine its business model (Venkatraman, *Netflix: A Case of Transformation for the Digital Future*, 2017).

Big data is robust, but big data plus big ideas are convertible. Netflix is a technology juggernaut; it built a platform that shapes what customers watch, not just how they watch, through its analytics, algorithms, and digital-streaming innovations that changed how customers watch movies and TV shows. However, this technology has always been in service of a unique point-of-view building (Taylor, 2018). This powerful data system creates a wealthy social system that influences the movies and shows members see, based in part on which shows they have liked in the past and what other subscribers see and like.

Every industry is facing a digital future; past rules will no longer apply. The future competitors will be those with digital capabilities, much as what Netflix has mastered over the last two decades to redefine entertainment.

Emirates Airlines Innovation Analytics (Marketing Techniques)

Emirates is a global airline, serving 154 airports in 82 countries from its hub in Dubai, United Arab Emirates. Emirates has been able to gain a competitive position and advantage in the marketplace since it started in 1985. Implementation of appropriate strategies has led to the exceptional performance, profitability, and success of Emirate Airlines. The reasons behind Emirates' success have been defined by their competitive advantages within the airline industry. These advantages are low labor costs, fuel-efficient and customer service-tailored aircraft fleet, avoidance of corporate alliances, aggressive sports marketing, and dedication to premier in-flight customer service. Their most prominent advantage is their lower labor costs that allow Emirates to lower their ticket prices and invest more money in aircraft upgrades and marketing. Emirates Airlines is a significant competitor for many global companies, and it is now the world's fourth-largest airline by international traffic. Emirates disrupts a market before they are disrupted through many factors; they use "Design Thinking" for complex problems and finding optimal solutions. They focus on velocity, the speed at which a plan comes to completion. They use their own business models. The co-creation factor is to develop solutions jointly with customers. The transparency involves operating in a way to make it easy for other stakeholders to see what is planned and the actions performed. The platform which Emirates takes as an approach to digitization enables it to control changes better and makes future initiatives more comfortable by having the ability to predict how customers will react to changes to the experience. Emirates does a significant number of surveys and focus groups on understanding what reduces the traveling experience. It helps with the accuracy of the ability to predict how changes will be perceived (Kerravala, 2015). The airline has developed an international reputation based on their excellent customer service, loyalty, value, and luxury, and has been awarded Best Airline in the World by Skytrax four times (Skytrax, 2016). In the current era, digital innovation is disrupting markets with extraordinary speed.

Efforts are made by Emirates to achieve these accolades concerning their competitive advantages in marketing and business strategy: concerning growth, the airline is the fastest in the world and has posted an average annual net profit progression of 20% (Jammoul, 2013). Emirates Airlines claim their rapid growth is mainly in the ability of their employees to understand how the social world is related. They expand on this theory in their belief that adjusting to customers' needs is structured around outside factors such as global economics, trade and politics, shifting populations, diversity, and sustainability. The advantages that make Emirates globally competitive are their central hubs located in Dubai, which are an ideal halfway point that connects the Western world (United States, Europe) to the Eastern world (India, China, Australia). Emirates uses objectives to avoid corporate alliances to reduce decision-making delays: their quick and aggressive responses to global financial market trends, in addition to their constant attentiveness and technological evolution concerning customer service, loyalty programs, and in-flight amenities.

Company image is identified by luxury, top-class customer service, efficiency, and value to provide consistently low prices by taking advantage of the UAE's strong economy and low labor prices. That image generates internationally recognized marketing campaigns through large sports teams and clever adverts. Overall, it has a very recognizable and consistent brand image that is attractive to all types of consumers. Emirates has become a globally well-known brand for many reasons; one of the most recognizable reasons is their aggressive marketing campaigns throughout the sports and entertainment world. Emirates company considers itself the most recognized airline in the sports world (Emirates Group, 2016). They are currently heavily involved with European Football through FA Cup and benefice sponsorship, PGA Tour golf, Formula 1 racing, Americas Cup sailing, horse racing, and significant sports leagues. Emirates' deals demonstrate polarizing marketing strategy and are only possible because of its ability to create massive revenues continuously and its independent business philosophy.

Strategically, Emirates sees growth potential in every facet of their business plan. They have broken things down to the basics and understood that customer satisfaction is derived from a straightforward aspect: customer service. Emirates has worked tirelessly to create influential customer service-related business culture while also actively investing in customer service technology to ensure widespread consistency. In respect to customer service technology, Emirates has invested in Knowledge-driven In-flight Service (KIS), which monitors the personal qualities of passengers on board. KIS uses server-based tablets to store passenger information, and analyze the data to develop a strong understanding of an individual's travel expectations, thus allowing the flight cabin-crew to provide more focused and personalized service. Emirates' excellent customer service reputation has ranked Emirates the top airline in the world for customer service with a score of 92.3% (Skytrax, 2016).

With respect to marketing strategies used by Emirates Airlines, Emirates Skywards members and their travel companions are enabled to access the award-winning lounges via a "pay-to-access" program and give families and group travelers the option to pay for advanced seat selection. They also revamped Emirates Business Rewards, the loyalty program for corporate customers. Future business for Emirate Airlines will be digitally integrated into the ecosystem of partners, suppliers, and with Dubai, offer more personalized customer experiences, and be enabled by a new suite of the latest technologies, including automation, robotics, and biometrics.

Amazon and Souq.com Innovation Analytics (Customers Database)

A decade ago, the availability of an online marketplace was an unimaginable thought; in 2005, an online marketplace "Souq.com" was created in the United Arab Emirates to become one of the most popular portals and redefined technology. It became a leading e-commerce marketplace company in the Middle East that has recently been acquired by Amazon.

After Souq came into its own as an independent entity in 2009, their focus was on retail, and their hard decision was to be able to meet customer expectations and grow the B2C (business-to-consumer) function; they started since then finding out what the customers want, and how they can adapt. This period in Souq's life cycle was a turning point for the company, but building up and transforming the website's product catalog was, at the time, a rather robust process for everyone involved at the startup. This was just the start of Souq's transformation into the Middle

East e-commerce giant it is today; as soon as the company felt it had improved the experience of the shopper on its website, they began to look at improving whatever happened post-click (Thomas, 2018), and that resulted in significant investments being made in payment, logistics, after-sales, and other such areas of the customer journey. Today, Souq.com features 8.4 million products and attracts 45 million visits per month. Souq.com also realizes that coming up with special events—such as Mobile Mania and White Friday, the equivalent of America's Black Friday—is one effective way to spruce up even more business.

Dubai being its headquarters has helped Souq.com knack for technology, media, and marketing and indeed helped the team scale greater heights. Also, people getting connected with mobiles helped Souq.com build its brand further, primarily through social media channels. Customer's needs and expectations have changed dramatically in recent years; 80% of customers shop through their mobile phone, so Souq focused on enhancing its mobile app's performance and usability. The six critical values in Souq's culture are trust, fun, innovation, initiative, growth, and the "wow" factor based on data software connecting customers to business and supply chain in an online data process.

The e-commerce business model for Souq.com caters to the needs of local markets with commercial offices in Egypt, the Kingdom of Saudi Arabia, and Kuwait, and a technical and development center in Jordan. In respect to the Souq growth journey, it managed to raise many funds during that time before the alignment with Amazon; the two companies approached innovation and customer-centricity to fuel their respective businesses partnership exchanging database and market knowledge. From Amazon's perspective, they were looking to enter the Middle East as part of its international expansion—and Souq proved to be the perfect vehicle, both are driven by customers, invention, and long-term thinking. Through this acquisition, Amazon will help Souq to continue to innovate in all sorts of capacities; customers will see more choice, which is very clear, to tap into the global supply of Amazon, its merchant base, and the partners that they work with.

The benefit from the acquisition with Amazon will enable Souq to drive further growth, benefit from their technological investment, offer a more extensive product selection through worldwide sourcing, deliver an enhanced customer service experience, as well as continue Amazon's excellent track record of empowering sellers locally and globally, and Amazon's customers will remain the key focus. They will continue to deliver a seamless online shopping experience. Their aim is to combine technology with trade, potentially with point-of-sale services.

What makes Amazon the most innovative company of the current era is its technological innovation, marketing strategy, and most importantly, its business model. Amazon has grown from book-selling websites to logistics, consumer technology, cloud computing, and most recently, media and entertainment. As a result of its e-commerce business model, Amazon launched its services to more markets and expanding horizons. They increased their sales numbers and customers and hence revenue (Singh, Google, 2019).

The business strategy of Amazon consists of investing in technologies, enhancing its logistic applications, improving its web services by fulfillment capacity, M&A strategy, Amazon Web Services (AWS) segment, R&D activities in logistics, and experimenting with Fintech. AI is one tight area where, despite having many competitors, Amazon got a big draw. It is continuously focusing on AI and machine learning to enhance customer experience, as an example for that Amazon's partnership with Microsoft ensures collaboration for researching in AI, where they developed Cortana and Alexa to communicate service offer to the users. Amazon announced its Alexa everywhere in 2017, and amazingly, it became a massive success despite the presence of other top personal assistants in the market. During the last few years, Amazon made multiple acquisitions to strengthen its core e-commerce operations. Additionally, it also invested in technology companies such as Harvest.ai—a cybersecurity player—and Do.com—a software for meeting productivity needs.

Internationally, and for growing its e-commerce in the region, Amazon expanded its operations by acquiring other businesses such as Souq.com in the Middle East. Recently, Amazon made their first acquisition of 2018, their second-biggest ever, in a deal valued more than $1 billion purchasing Ring, a video doorbell maker who shows their interest in robust home security to flourish their Amazon key service. Amazon has been experimenting with Fintech initiatives and intends to become a prominent player in the Fintech segment (Singh, GreyB Services, 2019).

Airbnb Innovation Analytics (New Product Development)

Airbnb is an online marketplace that matches people who rent out their homes— "hosts"—with people who are looking for a place to stay—"guests." Airbnb uses controlled experiments to make decisions at every step of product development, from design to algorithms. They are important in shaping the user experience. Airbnb is a company with the most prominent digital products in the world today; it's known for the innovative ways they use their data.

Since its establishment in 2008, Airbnb has led the growth of the sharing economy by allowing thousands of people around the world to rent their homes or spare rooms. At the end of 2011, Airbnb was entering hyper-growth with 13 international offices and over a million nights booked in 182 countries (Kirkland, 2014). One of Airbnb's fundamental beliefs is that every employee should be empowered to make data-informed decisions. The reason behind this growth is keeping its product-market fit. This changed Airbnb's entire product strategy and opened them up to develop new business categories. Product-market fit is the only thing that matters for them; they believe that if nobody wants what you're selling, then you do not have a business. Moreover understanding that Airbnb's product was the trip gave the team the right constraints to focus on innovation that rolled up to the brand promise, even as the market shifts, they could not have done this without first understanding how the customer saw their product. This allowed them to see what kinds of brand and product extensions were believable to customers and fit into their brand.

Establishing product-market fit can be incredibly challenging and requires much strategic planning around any intended users; the better you know them, the more clearly you understand their needs and motivations, the better you can optimize your product for them. Companies that understand their users better than their competitors can develop a product that's better fit for their market (Mandelli, 2018), which applies to the NPD concept. As the platform expands and spreads around the world, the data scientists at Airbnb are continually identifying and improving pain points to keep the end to end-user experience frictionless and positive. It is easy to focus on the happy user, the "correct" user path. Product analytics becomes a straightforward, reductive process when everyone does everything right, and everything goes well. You have your product funnel, and you track conversions from point to point.

The user journey is complicated; using data in the product development process is difficult because your users and their journeys are far from straightforward. This is the crux of why product analytics is crucial: robust and data-driven product teams will have the insight to build products that better serve your users, outclassing your competitors. In this highly competitive space, inches matter, and any tool that can give product teams an edge becomes a force multiplier. Data, like Airbnb and others have shown, has become one of those things that can give product managers and their companies an edge. Consider again Airbnb and their relatively new Data University. Their approach to democratizing data is to spread the skills, letting each employee learn as much as is desired or necessary to interact with data.

Another essential aspect that Airbnb focuses on is using large-scale experiments to test new products and innovations to guide decisions. Airbnb recently ran an experiment to test the impact of a new landing page design on search engine ranking and traffic. To conduct the experiment, Airbnb claimed the fact that it had landing pages with different URLs for different markets (San Francisco, Boston, New York, etc.). This meant that they could randomize the different URLs to include the new design or not, thereby isolating the design's effect on search engine traffic; by doing that, they were able to show that the new design was a success; the new landing page turned out to drive an increase of ~3.5% in search traffic, an improvement corresponding to tens of millions of incremental visitors per day for the platform (Fossett, 2018). Based on these findings, Airbnb launched a new design for all markets. Airbnb is based on the idea of the sharing economy, which is being celebrated for cities. People all over a city, in 60 seconds, can become microentrepreneurs.

Alibaba Strategy (Investing in People Knowledge)

Recognizing the power of data, Alibaba, a Chinese online and mobile commerce company, has created an open culture based on information sharing and transparency. Its vision is based on technology to buy, sell, finance, and deliver goods on its digital platforms around the world. Alibaba (BABA) is an online retailer; its business model is different from the leading e-commerce businesses in the United States. Whereas Alibaba is divided into three core businesses: Alibaba, Taobao,

Tmall, all three e-commerce websites serve to connect various types of buyers and sellers, allowing Alibaba to act as a middleman in China's emerging e-commerce industry (Blystone, 2019). From e-commerce and payments systems to cloud services and AI, there are few sectors left in which Alibaba hasn't already established a strong presence.

With respect to making vast piles of money and investing billions, Alibaba has also become a great example of success united with responsibility. Alibaba has developed a relaxed culture in which employees are the primary focus. Mentorship has been actively encouraged, and employees are often switched among the company's multiple divisions to broaden their experience (Mittal, 2018).

This culture, which values entrepreneurship, innovation, and service, facilitates the sharing of data efficiently across the organization. Alibaba attempts to educate all of its employees about big data. Alibaba believes those in charge of commercial operations should also be familiar with data analysis and, as such, provides necessary training. As a reason, in many companies, business intelligence and other departments are divided, making it difficult to link data analysis with daily operations. Also, the company's policies and procedures are prepared to promote and encourage innovation; the company seeks to unleash each employee's full potential by giving employees enough space to innovate. For example, under the company's "horse race" program, employees are encouraged to submit ideas to a committee. Approved ideas then become projects that are pursued with adequate resources and funding (IBM, 2014).

References

Blystone, D. (2019, May 29). *Understanding the Alibaba Business Model*. Retrieved from investopedia: https://www.investopedia.com/articles/investing/062315/understanding-alibabas-business-model.asp.

IBM, I. (2014) *Innovative Analytics-How the World's Most Successful Organizations Use Analytics to Innovate*. New York: IBM Institute for Business Value.

Jeff Fossett, D. G. (2018, November 5). *Using Experiments to Launch New Products*. Retrieved from Harvard Business Review: https://hbr.org/2018/11/using-experiments-to-launch-new-products.

Kerravala, Z. (2015, December 7). *Emirates Airline Outlines Its Strategy for Innovation at Cisco's IoT World Forum*. Retrieved from Network World: https://www.networkworld.com/article/3012352/emirates-airline-outlines-its-strategy-for-innovation-at-ciscos-iot-world-forum.html.

Kirkland, R. (2014, November). *The Future of Airbnb in Cities*. Retrieved from Mckinsey & Company: https://www.mckinsey.com/industries/travel-transport-and-logistics/our-insights/the-future-of-airbnb-in-cities.

Mandelli, A. (2018, January 26). *Intelligent Use of Data in Product Development Differentiates Successful Companies*. Retrieved from SnowPlow: https://snowplowanalytics.com/blog/2018/01/26/intelligent-use-of-data-in-product-development-differentiates-successful-companies/.

Mittal, T. (2018, February 13). *How the Alibaba Group Grew from a Small Apartment to a Global e-Commerce Giant.* Retrieved from YOURSTORY: https://yourstory.com/2018/02/the-story-behind-the-alibaba-group.

Singh, V. (2019). *Google.* Retrieved from Greyb: https://www.greyb.com/amazon-business-strategy/.

Singh, V. (2019). *GreyB Services.* Retrieved from greyb: https://www.greyb.com/amazon-business-strategy/.

Taylor, B. (2018, July 18). *To See the Future of Competition, Look at Netflix.* Retrieved from Harvard Buisness Review: https://hbr.org/2018/07/to-see-the-future-of-competition-look-at-netflix.

Thomas, A. S. (2018). *Making History (Literally): Souq.com CEO Ronaldo Mouchawar.* Retrieved from Enterprenuer Middle East: https://www.entrepreneur.com/article/294267.

Venkatraman, N. V. (2016, April 16). *Explorer.* Retrieved from www.medium.com: https://medium.com/@nvenkatraman/netflix-a-case-of-transformation-for-the-digital-future-4ef612c8d8b.

Venkatraman, N. V. (2017, April 16). *Netflix: A Case of Transformation for the Digital Future.* Retrieved from www.medium.com: https://medium.com/@nvenkatraman/netflix-a-case-of-transformation-for-the-digital-future-4ef612c8d8b.

WordPress. (2019, May 17). *Data Science.* Retrieved from Data scientist insights: https://datascientistinsights.com/2013/01/29/six-types-of-analyses-every.

Chapter 3

Business Predictive Analytics: Tools and Technologies

Dustin White
University of Nebraska at Omaha

Contents

Introduction

Working with data, it is best practice to explore the data available before deciding on a specific technique or method to analyze that data. Similarly, it is essential to understand the tools available to the data analyst prior to diving into a project. Some tools or software packages are designed with beginning analysts in mind, while others require significant technical expertise. When choosing a tool, it is helpful to consider not only the goals of the project, but also the intended data consumer.

This chapter is designed to provide a high-level description of several prominent classes of tools in business analytics. Each description will contain the following:

1. *Functionality*: What can they do? Major capabilities of each tool class will be discussed here, emphasizing cases in which one class is typically more useful than the others.
2. *Weaknesses*: When should this tool be avoided? Are there barriers to use?
3. *Intended audience*: What type of audience would benefit most from the consumption of resulting data products? What level of technical expertise enables consumption of the product? Are there additional expectations when consuming the data product?

Each class of tool will be described generally in order to facilitate comparison between the types of tools and the needs of various products. The groups to be considered are:

1. Business Intelligence (BI) Software
2. Open-Source Analytics Tools
3. Proprietary Analytics Tools

Business Intelligence Software is typically designed to aid in the consumption of prepared data and does not require a significant technical training. On the other hand, **Open-Source Analytics Tools** and **Proprietary Analytics Tools** typically expect higher levels of technical proficiency and can be utilized to consume prepared data or to facilitate the preparation of data for consumption. The primary difference between the two is that Proprietary Analytics Tools are typically provided at a cost and provide support to users, while Open-Source Analytics Tools are most often free, but offer little support outside of documentation.

While this chapter will not provide coverage of all possible tools, it will endeavor to provide valuable information about some of the most prominent tools available. The end of this chapter will provide a case study for the use of the Microsoft Power platform.

Learning Outcomes

1. Demonstrate knowledge of available data tools.
2. Identify the requirements of a specific business problem relative to selecting the appropriate tool for that problem.
3. Identify the appropriate tool for a business problem.
4. Familiarize the reader with the creation and use of data dashboards in Microsoft Power BI.

Business Intelligence (BI) Software

Business Intelligence (BI) Software is designed to accommodate the needs of firms and teams as they design reports focused on information designed to be part of the decision-making workflow. These software suites are designed to be responsive, dynamic, and accessible after only elementary training and familiarization with the software itself. While some familiarity with the software is important, BI software is designed to make understanding of the data and business needs more important than software training.

Three major players (among many) in this area are Tableau Desktop, Microsoft Power BI Desktop, and Google's Data Studio (Tableau, 2019; Microsoft, 2019; Google, 2019). While many other options exist, these three platforms highlight the capabilities of BI software to transform data into insight. Additionally, each is designed to work with data from nearly any source, and to process data focused on diverse business applications.

Functionality

When using BI software, the user should expect functions to be focused primarily on the presentation of information through the available data. The tools provided should enable the user to visualize, quantify, and characterize information. This capability makes BI software valuable to users at all levels of data proficiency.

One of the most valuable characteristics of BI software is the ability to generate *dynamic* reports. Rather than creating static figures using data to be presented in a slide show, BI software instead encourages the user to combine visuals and statistics into a report-style format. Once the figures, tables, and values are arranged, the user can explore the data interactively by clicking on various elements in a visual or table in order to isolate that same group of observations in the other elements of the report.

A unique capability driven by interactive reporting is the possibility of addressing questions immediately when discussing the solution to business questions. When a question is asked about an outcome or specific demographic, the interactive report format allows the user to *immediately* drill down to address that question (provided that the report has been thoughtfully constructed). This capability can easily reduce the number of follow-up emails or meetings required to address specific concerns and is one of the most powerful capabilities of BI software suites.

Weaknesses

BI tools are not designed to handle all of the many ways in which data may need to be used. Some of the use cases in which other tools should typically be used include:

1. *Data cleaning*: Most BI software expects the data to be processed prior to being imported. Currently, Tableau Desktop is only available as part of the Tableau Creator software suite. The other piece of software included is Tableau Prep, a program specifically designed for preparing and cleaning data prior to creating reports. Microsoft Power BI and Google Data Studio each expect that data will be cleaned prior to use, as well. In those cases, the user could certainly consider tools such as Microsoft Excel or Google Sheets as candidates for data cleaning software.
2. *Modeling*: BI software is designed to provide insights through carefully designed and presented reports. It is not designed to create powerful forecasting models or other robust statistical measures. This work is best done in other software although BI software often provides rudimentary trending and forecasting options.

Intended Audience

While nearly any business or individual can benefit from the versatile reporting that is created by BI software, it is especially valuable for individuals who regularly need to provide reports to managers, or who frequently present material to non-technical audiences. By presenting visual reports that can be adapted dynamically, users can benefit from the unique and simple presentation style facilitated by BI software.

Another tremendous advantage is that almost no technical expertise is required of the user. While it is of course necessary to understand the context and scope of the data being used to create the report, very little training is needed for an individual to become a skilled user of BI software. Even individuals with little to no statistical background and no programming experience can successfully implement BI reports using any of the software suites mentioned above.

Open-Source Analytics Tools

Open-source tools are more diverse and varied than BI software. Some tools, such as Dash (a tool built to use Python) or Shiny (a tool implemented using R), are designed to function similar to BI software, and allow users to create valuable dashboards or reports that can be presented to diverse audiences (Plotly, 2019; RStudio, 2019; Python Software Foundation, 2019; The R Foundation, 2019). Some tools, such as TensorFlow or Scikit-learn, are designed to implement highly technical statistical models that can be used to forecast or predict based on new observations (Abadi et al., 2015; Pedregosa et al., 2011). Other tools are focused on data cleaning, data collection, or research-oriented statistical modeling.

The greatest advantage, then, of open-source software is the versatility that it offers. For nearly any analytics project, there are tools that can improve the efficiency and effectiveness of that project. For example, an open-source data analytics pipeline to understand the way that people feel about a product sold online (sentiment analysis) using tools built on the Python programming language might look like the following:

1. Use Scrapy (open-source library for scraping websites) to collect customer comments or reviews (Scrapinghub, 2019).
2. Use Pandas (open-source library for handling data sets) to build the structure of the data (McKinney, 2010).
3. Use NLTK or spaCy (both open-source libraries for processing text) to identify keywords and sentiment in comments/reviews (Bird, Klein, and Loper, 2009; Honnibal and Montani, 2017).
4. Use one of many open-source plotting tools to visualize trends.
5. Use Statsmodels or scikit-learn (open-source libraries for statistical analysis and prediction) to create statistical models (Seabold and Perktold, 2010; Pedregosa et al., 2011).
6. Use Dash (open-source library for creating interactive web-based dashboards) to create a report on the results of the study (Plotly, 2019).

Functionality

Open-source software is immensely flexible in functionality. There are available software options for nearly any need, ranging from operating systems allowing for the implementation of an analytics pipeline to libraries to implement a single statistical model or generate a single type of visual. Because these are tools that are developed by individuals and organizations, and are subsequently licensed for use in other contexts, the existence and availability of an open-source tool is based almost entirely on the existence of a business need and the willingness of the developer to collaborate with other individuals on the use and development of that tool.

It is difficult to scope the functionality of open-source tools, but it is reasonable to assume that if there is a specific functionality that is needed in more than a single use case, there is likely an open-source tool to accommodate that need.

Weaknesses

The weaknesses of open-source software result directly from its greatest strengths. Open-source software is typically created and maintained by individuals or organizations who created the tool for their own use. The tools that these groups design expect much more of the end-user than software such as Tableau or Power BI. For example, libraries of code based on Python or R are nearly always designed with an expectation that the user be proficient in Python or R. Users who are not proficient in the programming language on which a tool is designed are simply left behind. For statistical models and libraries, individuals are also assumed to have sufficient statistical knowledge to implement the models without assistance.

Open-source software is created to solve specific problems. When those problems are resolved, many open-source projects cease to be maintained. Users are left to either maintain the project on their own or to move on to a newer project or library. This can be a serious drawback where a data project depends on stability and low-cost maintenance.

Interestingly, the strength of open-source software is also a weakness. It can become difficult to find the right library or software platform among the many options available. In order to find the right tool, a user needs to know what to look for. This problem is magnified when the user is not yet proficient in either programming or statistics, and therefore not prepared to search for technical terms that might reduce the number of search results.

While significant weaknesses exist within the open-source model, open-source software dominates data science. Firms and institutions ranging from Google and Facebook to government bodies and non-profits depend on these tools daily to drive decision-making processes.

Intended Audience

The intended audience for Open-Source Analytics Tools is best described as technically skilled and willing to design a custom workflow tailored to specific needs. The user needs to be technically skilled because, unlike with BI software, it is typically necessary to build out the tools used on an open-source platform. For example, while Google shares the TensorFlow deep learning library under an open-source license, the user must create a learning model using a compatible programming language and integrate that model with data in order to gain any value from TensorFlow for his or her own projects.

Again, the user must also be willing to design the workflow. In BI software, reports can be generated by dragging and dropping elements onto a canvas. In open-source software, it is expected that users will have to design each element of the interface using code. Dash and Shiny provide very similar functionality to BI software, yet each require the user to programmatically describe the design of the dashboard or report.

Where BI software is like eating at a restaurant, using open-source software is comparable to cooking a gourmet meal at home. With open-source software, the "flavor" can be tailored precisely, but at the cost of greater effort in training and implementation.

Proprietary Analytics Tools

Proprietary Analytics Tools, like open-source tools, are not an entirely distinct class of software. It is entirely reasonable to consider proprietary BI software to be a subset of this class. Due to the prevalence and usefulness of BI software, however, it is best to consider the two separately. For our purposes, Proprietary Analytics Tools will be compared more closely with the Open-Source Analytics Tools discussed previously.

The obvious difference between proprietary and open-source tools is the difference in ownership of the platform. Proprietary tools are licensed and maintained by firms whose business model is built on supplying a tool or suite of tools to users for a cost (either to buy the software or to host it). Examples of this business model are Tableau (in the BI arena) and Microsoft Office. On the other hand, open-source tools are liberally licensed and are maintained as part of the business process of firms or users. These tools are not typically intended as the product from which the firms or users generate revenue.

Functionality

The functionality of proprietary tools varies greatly, ranging from BI software platforms such as the Tableau suite to established statistical analysis tools such as SAS, STATA, or SPSS. Focusing on the statistical analysis tools (we have already discussed Tableau above), the primary advantages of proprietary tools over their open-source counterparts are ease of use and professional support availability.

1. *Ease of use*: Proprietary statistical analysis tools (like SPSS and STATA) make heavy use of graphical interfaces to streamline the process of performing statistical analysis. For example, both SPSS and STATA provide drop-down menus containing options for conducting many traditional and contemporary statistical models by simply clicking the desired model and specifying necessary parameters in the windows provided. This contrasts with the need to manually code each model in open-source analysis tools. The daunting prospect of learning to code is a prominent reason for analysts and researchers to choose proprietary software over open-source alternatives.

2. *Professional support*: One of the single greatest strengths of proprietary analysis tools is the investment of the licensing firm or organization into creating an ecosystem surrounding the various tools and platforms. For example, Tableau, SAS, and STATA each offer hours of free training videos on their respective websites, as well as documentation regarding the use of the platforms. These materials are kept up to date as new releases of the software are published, ensuring that users can conveniently access training on new features as they become available. This stands in stark contrast to open-source tools, where updates often cause short-term harm due to changes that are not well documented or publicized by the team of individuals supporting software at no cost to users.

Weaknesses

The greatest weakness of Proprietary Analytics Tools is the cost of these tools, and the reduced ability of small teams and firms to make use of them due to the high cost of access. For example, the SAS Analytics Pro software is listed at $10,010 for a single-seat license at the time of writing. STATA lists a minimum price of $1,595 for a perpetual license for business use, and Tableau lists a minimum price of $840/year for a single user. In cases where more than one user or license is needed, prices increase further.

While the cost of these software platforms is designed to provide ease of use, clear documentation, software updates, and professional support, the cost is not trivial.

Intended Audience

The intended audience of Proprietary Analytics Tools are users who are willing to pay the cost of the proprietary tools in order to increase the ease of use and support provided. These users will typically work at firms that are capable of purchasing licenses, or in academic and/or government settings where discounted licenses are frequently offered. Wherever the cost is justified by the reduced learning curve and improved support, or where users are already familiar with some proprietary analytics tool, it is likely that proprietary tools will continue to be used.

The Right Tool for the Job

At this point, it is worthwhile to summarize when each tool would be ideal. The decision can be made by asking the user a short list of questions:

1. Is the data already processed, and you just need to build reports that can be easily maintained as the data updates over time?
2. Are you comfortable using programming languages or learning to program? Do you instead prefer menus?
3. Are you already familiar with any proprietary tools?

4. Do you need ready access to training provided by the maintainers of the tool?
5. Do you have funds to pay for proprietary tools?

If the answer to question (1) is "yes," then the user is most likely to benefit from access to BI software. Otherwise, if answers to (2) through (4) include preferences for menu-based tools, familiarity with proprietary tools, and ready access to training, and the answer to (5) is "yes," then the user is most likely to benefit from access to Proprietary Analytics Tools. In cases where the answer to (5) is "no," or where users are comfortable learning on their own, enjoy using programming languages, or are unfamiliar with any proprietary tools, the ideal choice is likely to be Open-Source Analytics Tools.

These questions do not provide universal solutions, and many choices will need to be made based on the context of project needs and other case-specific conditions. Preference should certainly be given to the availability of tools that are essential to the completion of necessary steps or types of analysis. For example, it will be very difficult to implement many cutting-edge forms of analysis in any platform other than Open-Source Analytics Tools. It will also be difficult to work with many legacy data structures outside of the heavily supported proprietary analytics platforms. Careful consideration of the needs of a particular project should occur before committing to any platform or software.

Case Study: Microsoft Power BI and Football Attendance

Understanding patterns and trends is a powerful capability in any industry. By linking data to information about changes in an industry or the economic environment, firms can generate insights that lead to increased retention and engagement with customers.

While few firms are eager to share the kind of information that allows for a study of these concepts in the open, sports can provide a refreshing insight into the ways in which consumption patterns may change over time. In the sports industry, it is straightforward to uncover attendance measures (or even television viewership levels!) and associate that information with the outcomes of matches or competitions.

Information such as the aggregated outcomes of a season can be interpreted as a measure of product quality. In this light, observing match attendance in sports combined with match outcomes (or aggregated measures of performance like win percentage or league position) provides an intriguing case study in the effect of quality on consumption over time.

This section breaks down the construction of a dashboard to explore attendance at European football matches. The dashboard will be supplemented by performance measures for clubs in the English Premier League during recent seasons in order to explore the relationship between performance and attendance in football.

Getting Started with Football Attendance Data

The data for this case can be found in a GitHub repository dedicated to this chapter: https://github.com/dustywhite7/attendance-reports. The CSV, or file containing the data, can be found at the following URL: https://raw.githubusercontent.com/dustywhite7/attendance-reports/master/football-attendance-europe.csv. The data to be used was collected from European-football-statistics.co.uk and fbref.com (European Football Statistics, 2019; Sports Reference LLC, 2019).

The data file contains five variables: country, position, team, average attendance, and year. Country indicates the country from which a record is drawn. Position indicates the rank of the record within a specific country's league that year. Team indicates the club to which the record belongs. Average attendance is the average number of fans attending a club's matches in the season of record (measured in thousands of fans). Year indicates which year/season the record belongs to.

Introducing Microsoft Power BI

Microsoft Power BI is an excellent tool that is widely available and inexpensive to use. While Power BI is a proprietary tool (and therefore has the support that is expected of Microsoft products), it is also available at no cost to desktop users (with Microsoft instead choosing to charge for generating and storing reports using the cloud-based version of the software as the revenue model for the platform). Power BI is available for use on any computer utilizing the Windows operating system, and can be downloaded at the following link: https://powerbi.microsoft.com/desktop/.

Once the data has been downloaded and Power BI has been installed, it is possible to quickly and easily start to learn from data by creating dynamic dashboards in Power BI.

Importing Data

In order to begin the import process, choose the "Get Data" button from the "Home" control ribbon. Click on the icon, and a pop-up menu will appear where it is possible to choose the type of data to connect to (as shown in Figure 3.1). Open the drop-down menu by clicking on the text rather than the icon to choose a data type without entering the pop-up menu.

The data for this case is stored in a file with the extension ".csv," so the correct selection is "Text/CSV."

A file browser will open once the data type has been selected and confirmed, as in Figure 3.2. Select the file to connect to the report. For example, the file stored on GitHub is named "football-attendance-europe.csv," so that is the file name that should be selected to import into the report. When selecting a file, Power BI will present a preview of the data in that file, like the preview shown in Figure 3.3. The intent of this screen is to ensure that the data being imported is the correct data.

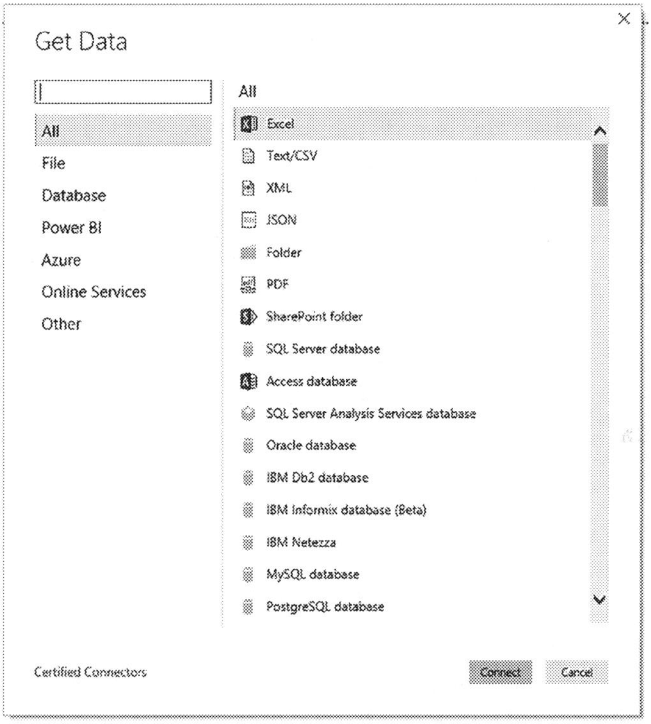

Figure 3.1   File type selection screen.

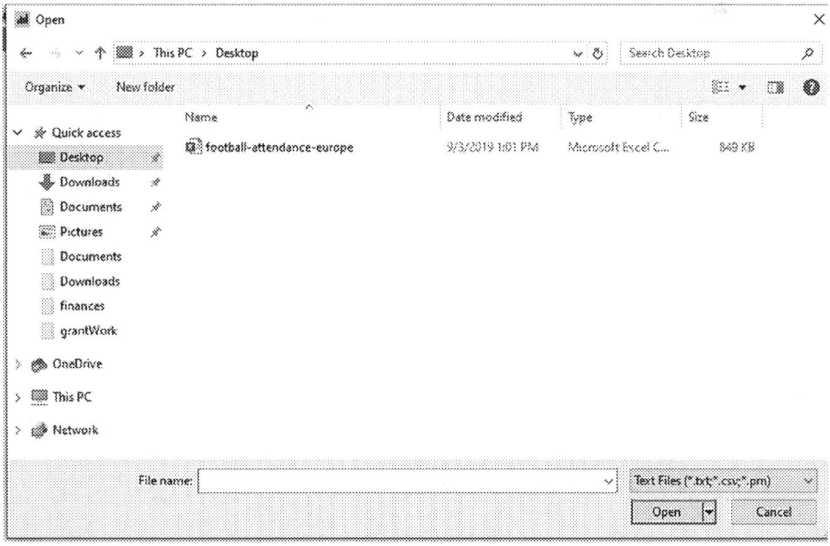

Figure 3.2   File selection screen.

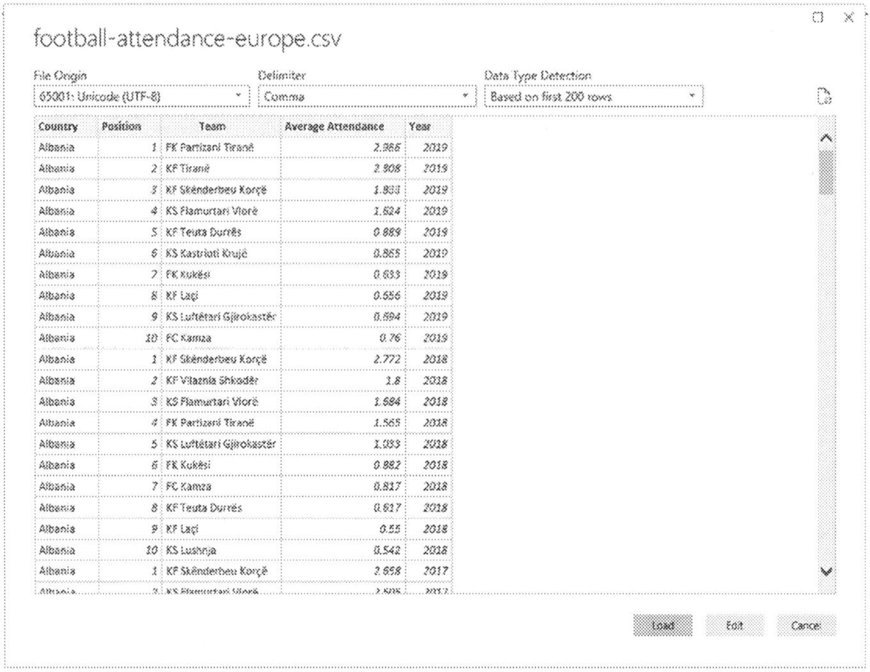

Figure 3.3   Data verification screen.

This verification prior to importing data becomes important in the case that data files are very large, since large files will take a significant amount of time to load into memory. The user can choose to either edit or load data. If everything looks right, select "Load." If modifications are needed, then select "Edit." Because many football clubs have names with local characters, be sure to select "65001: Unicode (UTF-8)" as the file origin option while importing the data.

After selecting "Load," the columns (or fields) of our data will be available on the main page of the report. The column names will be presented in the "Fields" column at the extreme right of the window. The fields should be the same as those in Figure 3.4.

Creating a Visual

Now that the data is accessible via Power BI, it needs to be translated to a visual medium in order to provide accessible information to viewers. The pre-built visuals available in Power BI can be selected in the "Visualizations" tab on the right-hand side of the Power BI interface, shown in Figure 3.5. Additionally, users who prefer to create their own visuals can do so by incorporating Python or R code through widgets providing integration with the two popular languages.

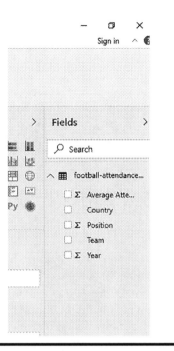

Figure 3.4   The power BI fields list.

Figure 3.5   Power BI visualizations and fields.

To start exploring the football data, select the line chart widget from the Visualizations tab. At this point, a blank visual appears on the canvas, and fields appear under the Visualizations tab through which the user can incorporate fields into the visual. By adding the "Year" field to "Axis," "Team" to "Legend," and "Average Attendance" to "Values," a preliminary visual can be generated. See Figures 3.6 and 3.7.

The figure generated (and shown in Figure 3.8) now shows team-season records across all included countries. This visual contains approximately 22,000 records! Because of the number of observations, not all records will be shown by default. While the outliers are easy to find, it would be more useful to be able to filter the data so that meaningful insights can be generated, and to guarantee that the points of interest will be rendered on the visual.

Creating a Filter

In order to filter the data, Power BI provides the "Slicer" class of widgets. After clicking on the "Slicer" button under "Visualizations," the user simply needs to drag a field into the "Field" area provided by the slicer. Start by selecting country as the field to slice. Choosing a country from the newly created list of options will

Figure 3.6   Providing data for the line chart.

Figure 3.7   Choosing average value as measure.

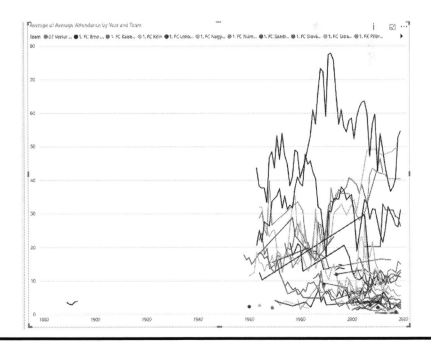

Figure 3.8   The first line chart.

filter the visual on the canvas to include only observations from the selected country. For example, ticking the box next to "England" will reduce the observations in the scatter chart to only the subset of records for English clubs. The slicer and its options are shown in Figure 3.9.

Any number of slicers can be created on a canvas. Creating additional slicers is only a matter of making space on the canvas, adding the slicer, and providing another field that can be used to further refine the results of figures on the canvas.

Club Performance and Attendance

With information about many years, countries, and clubs available through this first data set, it might be useful to supplement the data with additional information about the performance of clubs in each season in order to explore the relationship that club performance has with attendance. Additional data on the 2000–2018 seasons of the Premier League (the football league and clubs associated with England in the data used above) is provided in the GitHub repository and is accessible at the following URL: https://raw.githubusercontent.com/dustywhite7/attendance-reports/master/epl-season-rankings.csv.

Linking Data

One of the most powerful features of BI software is the capability to blend data from two sources without having to work with SQL (Structured Query Language) or other code. In this case, information regarding team performance can be combined with attendance

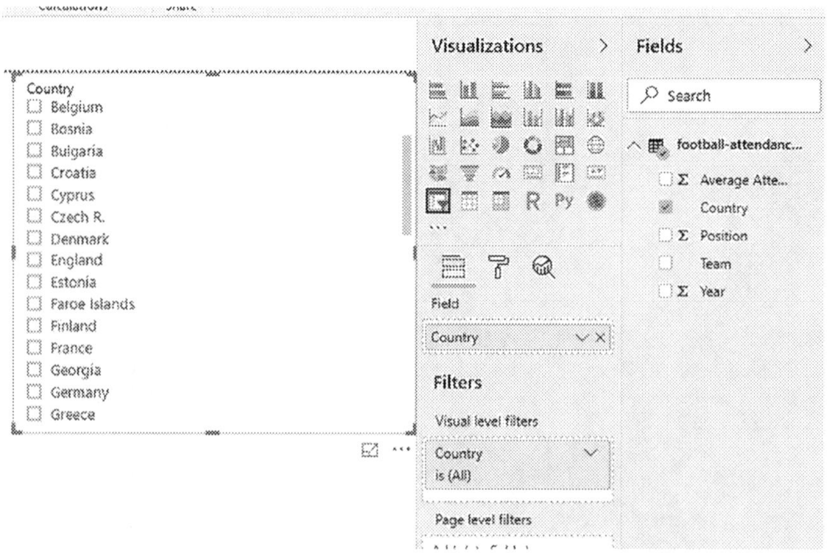

Figure 3.9 Creating a slicer.

figures to provide insights into the relationship between season-level results and attendance. To combine data sources, both CSV files need to be imported into Power BI per the instructions provided above. When both data sets are imported properly, each should appear in the "Fields" tab on the far right of the screen.

The two data sources can be combined in the "Edit Queries" menu found in the "Home" ribbon at the top of the screen. Once a new window opens, an option is provided to "Merge Queries" in the ribbon of the new window. Be sure to click on the primary data source in the tab on the left of this window prior to clicking the "Merge Queries" button. At this point, a prompt is opened (see Figure 3.10) so that the user can select the way in which to blend the data sources.

A preview of the primary data source will appear in the top half of the screen, and the second data source can be chosen from the drop-down menu in order to preview the secondary data source in the bottom half of the screen. The previews are shown in order to allow the user to select the columns that will match rows between the data sources. In the two data sources provided above, each row is a unique country-year-team combination. To blend the data sources, these columns need to be selected in each of the preview windows *in the same order.* In the first preview window, click on the "Country," "Year," and "Team" column titles while holding down the Ctrl button on the keyboard. Next, click on the same columns *in the same*

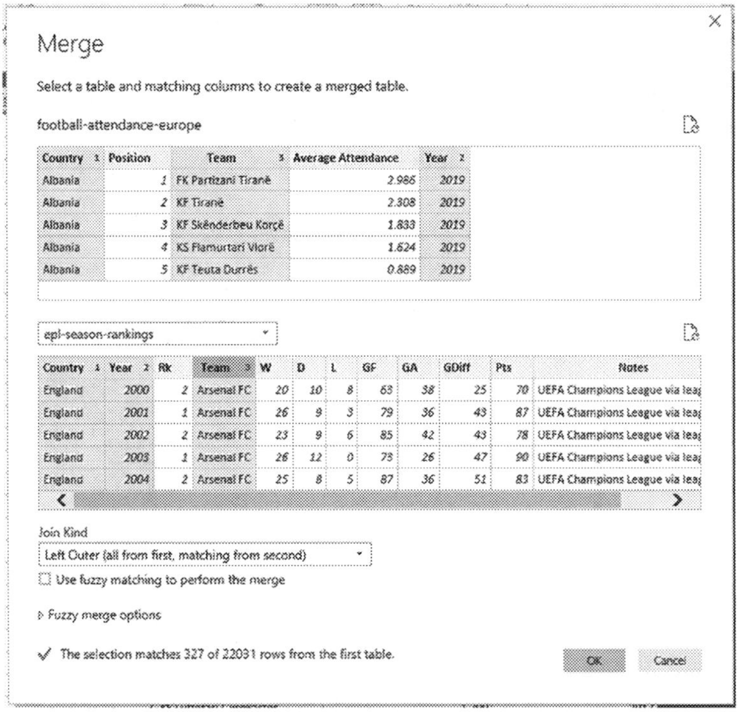

Figure 3.10   Merging data sources.

order in the second preview window. At this point, a small text field at the bottom of the window will indicate how many matches exist between the two data sources. In the case of the football data, there should be 327 matches (all the English club records between 2000 and 2018).

After clicking "OK," the user is returned to the "Edit Queries" screen. At this point, all of the merged columns are combined into a single column in the preview window. As shown in Figure 3.11, the user should click the diverging arrows in the column heading, then select all of the columns of interest and click "OK." At this point, the merger can be finalized by clicking "Close & Apply" in the top-left corner of the window.

Looking for Relationships

On the main canvas screen, all merged fields should appear under the primary data source in the "Fields" tab on the right of the screen. Any of the available fields can now be used to create visuals or tables combining the data from the two sources.

The increased flexibility of multiple data sources becomes apparent when comparing club performance with attendance figures. To do so, create a scatter chart on the canvas with "Position" and "Rk" (representing rank in the league table during a given season) in the "Details" box, "Rk" in the "X Axis" box, and "Position" in the "Y Axis" box. Be sure to choose the "Average" rather than "Sum" of both "Position" and "Rk" on the axes in order to maintain the clarity of the visual.

The plot should show a clear positive correlation: a higher rank in attendance is correlated with a higher rank in the league table! To further illustrate this point, the user can add a trend line using the options available in the "Analytics" portion of the "Visualizations" tab, as seen in Figure 3.12.

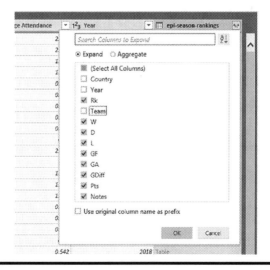

Figure 3.11   Expanding merged columns.

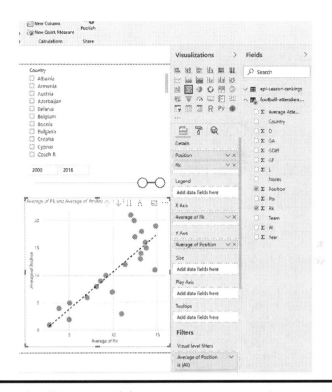

Figure 3.12   Visualizing merged data sources.

Debriefing

By creating interactive dashboards using BI software like Power BI, it is possible to explore many different research questions using a single interface, and without programming knowledge or expertise. These tools provide data accessibility for a much broader audience. They also facilitate the use of data for improved decision-making wherever data can be focused on a business application.

Experience with BI software enables users to provide dynamic and useful responses to active discussions during presentations. The interactivity of a dashboard allows the user to quickly adjust views of the data to respond to questions generated organically during a discussion of prior findings. For example, selecting the top-ranked teams in the scatter chart enables the user to observe those points on the average attendance line chart. Questions about specific years can be addressed by creating a year slicer and refining the view in the dashboard.

Dashboard creation is a high-demand skill due to the ability of dashboards to create flexible reporting tools. As more businesses rely on these tools to inform decisions, the value of dashboards and BI software to the enterprise will continue to increase.

Problem Set

1. What are two reasons to use Proprietary Analytics Tools? Think of a business case in which each of those reasons might apply.
2. When is it inappropriate to use BI software for a data project? What can be done to prepare that project to make use of BI software?
3. Write down a research question that can be answered using the data from this chapter together with BI software.
   a. What visuals and filters would be needed to address the question?
   b. Create the visuals and filters from part (a) using Microsoft Power BI (or another BI tool). What do the data suggest about the research question?
   c. What other data would help to address the research question?
4. Write a flowchart to decide whether a team should use BI Software, Open-Source Analytics Tools, or Proprietary Analytics Tools.
   a. Describe the data requirements of a research project (a work project, a class research project, or even a potential future project) and what the flowchart suggests about the appropriate tool for that project.
   b. Was this the same type of tool chosen for that project? If so, describe the usefulness of the tool in completing the project. If not, explain why another tool was chosen and whether it was effective in completing the project.
5. Choose a category of tool (BI software, open-source software, proprietary software) and find three tools that belong to the category and are used for similar tasks. Research the following questions for each tool:
   a. Who are the primary users of the tool?
   b. Why is this the preferred tool for its users?
   c. What is the cost to use the tool? Research and describe both financial costs as well as time to learn the tool.

Bibliography

Abadi, M., et al. (2015). *TensorFlow: Large-Scale Machine Learning on Heterogeneous Systems.* http://tensorflow.org/.

Bird, S., Klein, E., & Loper, E. (2009). *Natural Language Processing with Python: Analyzing Text with the Natural Language Toolkit.* Sebastopol, CA: O'Reilly Media, Inc.

European Football Statistics. (2019). *European Football Statistics.* http://european-football-statistics.co.uk/.

Google. (2019). *Data Studio Product Overview.* https://datastudio.google.com/overview.

Honnibal, M., & Montani, I. (2017). spaCy 2: Natural language understanding with bloom embeddings. *Convolutional Neural Networks and Incremental Parsing, 7*(1).

McKinney, W. (2010). Data structures for statistical computing in python. *Proceedings of the 9th Python in Science Conference, 445,* 51–56.

Microsoft. (2019). *Power BI Desktop-Interactive Reports: Microsoft Power BI.* https://powerbi.microsoft.com/en-us/desktop/.

Pedregosa, F., Varoquaux, G., Gramfort, A., Michel, V., Thirion, B., Grisel, O., Blondel, M., Prettenhofer, P., Weiss, R., Dubourg, V., & Vanderplas, J. (2011). Scikit-learn: Machine learning in python. *Journal of Machine Learning Research, 12,* 2825–2830.

Plotly. (2019). *Dash by Plotly.* https://plot.ly/dash.

Python Software Foundation. (2019). *About Python.* https://www.python.org/about/.

RStudio. (2019). *Shiny.* http://shiny.rstudio.com/.

Scrapinghub. (2019). *Scrapy | A Fast and Powerful Scraping and Web Crawling Framework.* https://scrapy.org/.

Seabold, S., & Perktold, J. (2010). Statsmodels: Econometric and statistical modeling with python. *Proceedings of the 9th Python in Science Conference, 57,* 61.

Sports Reference LLC. (2019). *Premier League Seasons.* https://fbref.com/en/comps/9/history/Premier-League-Seasons.

Tableau. (2019). *Tableau Desktop.* https://www.tableau.com/products/desktop.

The R Foundation. (2019). *R: What Is R?* https://www.r-project.org/about.html.

Chapter 4

Hospitality Analytics: Use of Discrete Choice Analysis for Decision Support

Pedro Longart
Higher Colleges of Technology

Contents

Introduction

Eating out of home has become an integral part of people's lives. This is because people have changed their attitudes about food and also due to an increase in disposable income (Capstick, 2011). Eating out normally takes place in restaurants, which have become an important part of our everyday lifestyles, and offers 'a place to relax and enjoy the company of family, friends, colleagues, and business associates' (Walker, 2014; p. 160).

There are many types of restaurants. A fine dining restaurant is one where a good selection of menu items is offered with a high level of service. Mehta and Maniam (2002) claimed that fine dining (or gourmet) restaurants are the most formal, fine dining experiences. Casual dining is more relaxed and could be part of one or a combination of ethnic, family and mid-scale casual. Although most family restaurants are seen as casual dining, some operations are targeting a more upscale customer. Ethnic restaurants base their ethnicity on the type of food served: Mexican, Indian, Chinese, Spanish, Italian, etc. Casual dining may include restaurants that are mid-scale in many countries (or considered as upscale in others) such as chains like TGI Friday's, Hard Rock Café, and Frankie and Benny's.

Due to this variety, choosing a particular context is challenging. A snack on the way to work could be considered as eating out. However, that can be considered as a low involvement, repetitive, routine customer decision. Eating out for leisure purposes entails complex phenomena. Consumers give many reasons for eating out, and those reasons may be compatible with how they live their lives. For example, for some people, as Charles and Kerr (1988) found, a proper meal is an occasion in which table manners are adhered to.

From the restaurateurs' perspective, they have a daunting task in working on a long list of aspects of their restaurants; therefore, a prioritisation of attributes by ascertaining attributes' importance is necessary. Some studies have attempted studying restaurant attribute importance, and hence, the first objective of this literature review is to analyse the various attempts that have been made to find out what attributes are more important for certain consumer segments and for certain occasions for eating out. A second objective focuses on the critical analysis of methodologies used for these investigations and to suggest a more suitable method for the purpose of understanding consumers' preferences in the context of choosing a restaurant.

Literature Review

Foundations of Consumer Research: Cognitive Approach

One of the cornerstones of the cognitive approaches of consumer research and most theories of choice is the presumption of a rational consumer. Hargreaves-Heap et al. (1992) started with the main conundrum for studying choice: What makes a choice rational? They explain that rationality is a matter of means, not ends. These rational actions can be represented as those of individuals seeking to maximise utility – or expected utility (Hargreaves-Heap et al., 1992). If a consumer is hungry, and he/she has two choices, he will most likely go for the choice that will better satisfy hunger. Utility can be defined as the measure of how the hunger is satisfied. If I have objective measures such as calories, and the information about the caloric content is available, then there is objective utility involved. However, in many cases, utility is subjective; then it depends – amongst other things – on preferences. This is the topic studied by the theory of subjective expected utility (SEU) that according to Simon (1986) is central to the body of prescriptive knowledge about decision making.

Behavioural Decision Theory

Theories of Choice

When investigating the behaviour of a large number of individuals making the particular decision of eating out and choosing a particular restaurant, the aggregate behaviour of restaurant patrons is the result of each individual decision. Ben-Akiva and Lerman (1985) explained that there is no universally accepted theory of choice that satisfies the requirements laid out above. A choice, they continue, is a sequential decision-making process that includes the following steps:

1. Definition of the choice problem
2. Generation of alternatives

3. Evaluation of attributes of the alternatives
4. Choice
5. Implementation.

In this context, the choice problem is that of a consumer deciding where to eat out, not for convenience, that is, lunch between working hours. His place of residence or stay will define the alternatives (restaurants available). The next step is about evaluation of the alternatives, and a discussion of alternatives will be included later in this literature review. The consumer needs to collect information about relevant attributes of that restaurant. In order to do that, the consumer applies a decision rule to arrive at a choice. Then, implementing the choice is obviously the meal itself. Thus as Ben-Akiva and Lerman pointed out, any specific theory of choice is a collection of procedures that encompass the following elements: the decision maker, alternatives, attribution of alternatives, and decision rules.

The Alternatives

Wright (1975) found that decision makers try to simplify their decision making and when studying models of decision making, a clear example is that of how alternatives are elicited. Shocker et al. (1991) characterised decision making as based upon hierarchical alternatives. Ben-Akiva called them a choice set. The universal set refers to the totality of all possible alternatives, which in this case may be the restaurant in a certain location, that is, London. This set is just a starting point as it is impossible to consider thousands of alternatives such as in the London restaurant scene. Then, there is a set that springs to the customer's mind; that means that they may remember them unaided. This has been called the evoked set (Howard, 1963), which comes from the awareness set, which is composed of evoked sets, inept sets and inert sets (Narayana and Martin, 1975). The model of Shocker et al. only considers the evoked set, which is also called the consideration set. They could also possibly be drawn from a list or restaurant guide (see External Alternatives). The definition from Shocker et al. appears to be more complete in separating awareness from consideration, indeed an important difference for marketers. In the context of restaurant decision making, it can be argued that the distinction is important and for that reason, Shocker et al.'s model will be preferred.

The consideration set is a reduction from the awareness set to a smaller set of alternatives (Gensch and Soofi, 1995). Horowitz and Louviere (1995) warned that 'using a consideration stage may lead to a misspecified model that would provide erroneous forecasts' (p. 40). However, in the case of restaurants, it is sensible to assume that consumers engage in an extensive information search to arrive at a decision. This is linked with the information processing theory, which is an approach in which 'the consideration set is formed and used by the consumer for subsequent purchase operations' (Roberts and Nedungadi, 1995). The choice set has a very strong influence upon the individual intention to choose a particular restaurant.

This was evidenced by the study of Davis and Warshaw (1991). Davis and Warshaw suggested that consumers employ screening procedures using decision rules, more particularly, non-compensatory rules to reduce the consideration set to a manageable size.

Decision Rules

The concept of utility is inextricably linked to decision rules. That means that consumers consciously or unconsciously assign values to the alternatives. That could mean the utility maximisation of satisfaction and minimisation of cost (or maximisation of value for money). Typically, consumers can only consider a small part of all the information available to them about a specific service. Heuristics are 'rules of thumb' (Shah and Oppenheimer, 2008) that individuals unconsciously apply to reduce the effort involved in decision making.

Decision rules have been traditionally seen as completely unrelated to impulsivity. Yet, as pointed out by Hsee and Tsai (2008), they are closely intertwined as most decision rules are antidotes to impulsive behaviour and entail some sort of self-control mechanism.

As for the choice criteria, Devetag (1999) distinguished between two types of heuristics: compensatory and non-compensatory. A heuristic is said to be compensatory if good values on some attributes can compensate for poor values on other attributes. On the contrary, a heuristic rule can be defined as non-compensatory if that compensation does not have effect. In compensatory behaviour, according to Statt (1997), the consumer uses more than one criterion to evaluate a product or service and there are two versions of this type of rules. The first and simpler version has the consumer as unconsciously adding the pluses and minuses of each alternative and the one with the most pluses wins. In the more complex version, the relevant attributes are weighted according to their importance for the consumer. Solomon (2007) described non-compensatory rules as 'choice shortcuts' in which people eliminate all options that do not meet the consumer's basic standards. Understanding these shortcuts is essential for a restaurateur as his/her restaurant may not even enter in a consideration set because of the nature of non-compensatory behaviour with regard to certain attributes and more particular features of that attribute, which are called levels of the attribute. That is, the restaurant may not reach the minimum threshold of that attribute (minimum level) to be considered by a decision maker. The concept of attribute level is discussed below.

Past Research on Restaurant Attributes

Cousins et al. (2002) pointed out that restaurant consumers base their decision for eating out on the type of experience that is sought. It can be argued that this experience has transcended the mere necessity to eat as discussed below. Macht et al. (2005) conducted a study on the hedonic pleasures of eating and concluded that indeed those pleasures are beyond food and nutrition and are shaped by features of the environment, social factors, and emotions. According to Mittal et al. (1998), the components of a service are evaluated by consumers separately. Several attempts have been made to establish what these aspects are within the restaurant setting. Campbell-Smith (1967) developed the concept of the meal experience with five different components that were later refined by Cousins et al. (2002). These components are food and drink, level of service, cleanliness-hygiene, value-for-money and ambiance. This model, as asserted by Wood (1994), has been very influential. Wood commented that the model has had a considerable effect on education in the hospitality industry, and also that it has initiated the application of practical marketing concepts in that industry.

The pursuit of leisure can arguably imply trying to maximise consumer utility. For this reason, it is maintained that consumers pursue the maximisation of utility for attributes that satisfy their needs and expectations. The different models of the meal experience attempt to offer an explanation of those factors which consumers may evaluate prior to making the decision to choose a particular restaurant. Indeed, research conducted on the meal experience has attempted to ascertain the relative importance of factors as considered by consumers since these may influence their decision. Several studies of these factors have brought about varied results. It should be noted that these investigations have conveyed different aims and objectives and have adopted different approaches. Whilst there are some similarities between attributes in the fast-food restaurant sector, there are also very important differences. To illustrate this point, in a study of fast-food restaurants, Mamalis (2009) found that the key critical success factors are adaptation to locality, food quality, service, facilities, 'Place to be' and sales incentive programme. Adaptation to locality may be critically important when restaurant chains have to cater to local tastes. Food quality, service and facilities are also elements of the meal experience in a fine dining restaurant, but key performance objectives of the operation such as speed are obviously more important in fast-food operations. Place to be refers to elements of ambiance, and includes elements of safety, which have not been mentioned in less casual dining environments. The last factor, the sales incentive programme, is particularly important for price-sensitive segments, such as the ones who regularly patronise fast-food restaurants. The implications of Mamalis's study may also affect sectors other than the fast-food industry, particularly for the increasing trend of globalisation of restaurant chains and the targeting of a customer who is brand conscious, even for dining out occasions. Another aspect is that of ethnic restaurants, those which portray a particular type of cuisine: Italian, Chinese, Greek, etc. Authenticity has been referred to as an attribute that is specifically linked to ethnic restaurants. Authenticity relates to both food and the environment and the degree to which it reflects the genuine taste and culture of the ethnic origin (Jang et al., 2011). Liu and Jang (2009) found that authenticity affects customer satisfaction, particularly when it relates to the perception of the food being authentic. Sukalakamala and Boyce (2007) extended the number of attributes that affect perceptions of authenticity to aspects such as interior décor, music, staff clothing, greetings, tableware/silverware and menu design.

There is extensive research on restaurant attributes in different geographical areas and with different customer segments. Some of these studies deserve attention, albeit briefly. Amongst these, Dulen (1999) and Susskind and Chan (2000) suggested that food, atmosphere and service are three major components of the restaurant experience. Ribeiro-Soriano (2002) studied four main attributes: food, service, cost and place (a combination of ambiance, location, facilities such as car parking and cleanliness-hygiene). The study confirms that food was the highest ranked with consumers over 60 years of age, ranking it significantly higher than any other attribute. Law et al. (2008) conducted a study of attributes for tourists in China and used the following classification of attributes and sub-attributes: food and beverage (portions, variety, quality, presentation); service (operating hours, diversity, speed and server's attitude); value for money; and environment (atmosphere, cleanliness, comfort, location and decoration), and they included an additional attribute, namely attraction (image, novelty, word-of-mouth, advertising). There was little elaboration in that research paper about the last attribute and it is arguable whether it is a restaurant attribute at all, as attraction may be considered to be a consequence of other restaurant attributes. Meng and Elliott (2008) referred to relationship marketing and communication as predictors of retention of loyal and satisfied customers based on the model of Kim et al. (2006). The latter authors proposed a measurement model of predicting relationship quality for luxury restaurants in South Korea and used the following classification for attribute dimensions: physical environment, customer orientation (service), communication, relationship benefits, price fairness and relationship quality. Narine and Badrine (2007) researched consumers eating out in Trinidad, West Indies, and they found similar aspects of the meal experience. In the study, food choices were influenced by health/nutritional benefits (60.8%), safety/sanitation (60.0%) and price of menu (55.8%). The celebration of a special occasion (60.8%) was the most popular reason for 'eating out'. In a research of attributes in Quick Service Restaurants (QSR), Harrington et al. (2013) supported other studies that indicate the general importance of the following restaurant attributes: (a) food safety, (b) cleanliness, (c) food quality, (d) speed of service, (e) perceived value of the food and drink items, (f) quality of service, (g) staff friendliness, (h) price, (i) variety of menu and (j) close travel distance. On the other hand, in a study of online customer reviews on restaurants (from the UK, USA, India, Germany, Italy, Norway, the Netherlands, Sweden, Switzerland and Spain), Pantelidis (2010) found that the most mentioned factors for customer satisfaction were food (96%), service (92%), ambiance (51%), price (29%), menu (27%) and design/décor (10%). An aspect worthy of investigation is the combined effects of restaurant attributes. So far, only Wall and Berry (2007) have addressed this topic in a study of the combined effects of the physical environment and employee behaviour, and found that the human element was significantly more important, as to an extent these 'humanistic clues' can make up for deficiencies in what they call 'mechanistic clues'. Andaleeb and Conway (2006) suggested that to satisfy customer expectations, restaurateurs ought to focus their efforts on service quality, price and food quality, in that order. Nonetheless, these authors acknowledged that this order is partly induced by the design of their methodology which is heavily focused on service quality. In another study, Namkung and Jang (2008) also ranked food first, followed by the physical environment and service. However, 'their study failed to consider price – an unfortunate omission – in the midst of an economic recession, given the likelihood that restaurant guests would have greater price sensitivity' (Pantelidis, 2010; p. 485).

From this discussion, it can be noted that the number of studies about restaurant attributes is overwhelming. For the constraints of space referred to, only an excerpt of the most influential – and/or cited – work regarding restaurant attributes have been discussed.

Ascertaining Attribute Importance

Challenges for Ascertaining Importance

The main limitations in ascertaining importance is that in the first place respondents are normally given a list rather than having the possibility of choosing what attributes they actually consider important; secondly, ascertaining importance isolated from the actual decision of selecting a restaurant seems like an unnatural task; thirdly, the description of an attribute does not offer enough information about what the attribute is about (this is defined more clearly when levels of the attribute are presented – see research design), and finally attribute importance ascertained by listing does not take into account the fact that price may influence attribute importance and that there may be a trade-off between price and the relative importance of an attribute. This means that for some consumers an attribute changes its relative importance if it attracts a higher price.

For all of the exposed above, it seems like it is about time that another approach is taken for ascertaining restaurant attribute importance, an approach that deals with those critical limitations. A set of methodologies, namely conjoint analysis, appears to offer a reasonable alternative as it looks as the natural trade-offs that consumers make.

Conjoint Analysis or Discrete Choice Analysis

Conjoint analysis refers to techniques used to estimate attribute utilities based on subjects' responses to combinations of multiple decision attributes (Louviere, 1988). Basically, conjoint analysis could also be called trade-off analysis because that is basically what the techniques are about. However, as highlighted by Louviere (1988), it must be clearly understood that conjoint analysis is not a single tool but a set of techniques that share some commonalities but also important differences. Orme (2010) distinguished between traditional conjoint analysis, developed in the 1970s, and conjoint analysis after the development of commercial software in the 1990s.

Orme (2010; p. 29) summed up the inherent limitations of conjoint analysis:

> Human decision making and the formation of preferences is complex, capricious and ephemeral. Traditional conjoint analysis makes some heroic assumptions… and that complex decision making can be explained using a limited number of dimensions. Despite the leaps of faith, conjoint analysis tends to work well in practice, and gives managers, engineers and marketers the insight they need to reduce uncertainty when facing important decisions. Conjoint Analysis is not perfect, but we do not need it to be.

Therefore, conjoint analysis allows for an approximation to reality, acknowledging that it is 'imperfectly apprehended' (Lincoln et al., 2011; p. 98).

In conjoint analysis, respondents choose attributes, for example, the portion which could be (a) small, (b) moderate and (c) large. If all the attributes with the corresponding levels are presented, that is called full profile. Green and Srinivasan (1990) noted that if the full-profile approach is used, it is important to limit the number of attributes and levels. Furthermore if the full profile is used, respondents tend to use simplification tactics if the information is overwhelming (Denstadli and Lines, 2007; Orme, 2010), and several authors have found that respondents may focus on salient attributes to the detriment of the rest. Because of the shortcomings of traditional conjoint, it was deemed necessary to examine the most popular conjoint analysis methodology, also known as discrete choice analysis (DCA).

Authors like Verma et al. (2002) and Louviere et al. (2010) argued that DCA is close but not the same as conjoint analysis. Verma and Thompson (1996) established a number of comparisons and based that differentiation on the fact that traditional conjoint analysis data are obtained in the form of ratings or rankings and that, in contrast, DCA places the respondents in simulated choice-making situations, in which they select choices they do not rate or rank. That is, DCA involves a single decision maker choosing one alternative amongst a small well-defined set (Ben-Akiva et al., 1997). Louviere et al. (2010) focused on the historical foundations of conjoint analysis, which are indeed different from DCA. However, there are so many similarities that it is possible to see DCA as an evolution of traditional conjoint analysis. To start with, influential conjoint research scholars such as Green et al. (2001) use the term 'Choice Based Conjoint' for DCA. Secondly, statistical models – also called estimation methods, for example, multinomial logit (MNL) models, or nested logit models developed from a DCA study relate service attributes to consumer preferences (Victorino et al., 2005). Thirdly, conjoint analysis is deemed to be inspired by scientific experimental design (Mazzocchi, 2008), in which the researchers manipulate the variables, in this case the attributes and their levels. In DCA, the research design takes the form of discrete choice experiments (DCEs). For instance, the decision maker responds to experimentally designed profiles of possible alternatives, in which each alternative has a different set of attributes (Verma and Thompson, 1996). Finally, the most popular software development organisation for conjoint analysis, Sawtooth Software ©, has developed several conjoint analysis solutions, with the most popular being Choice Based Conjoint (CBC) based on DCA theory. It should be noted that one of the main problems with traditional conjoint was with full profiles, as respondents have the task of rating, whereas that problem is minimised with discrete choices as respondents just have to choose a natural human task.

Conjoint Analysis in Restaurant Attributes Research

Conjoint analysis is a widely used methodology in the service industry, including hospitality and tourism. It can be noted that the studies in the context of restaurants of Koo et al. (1999), Verma and Thompson (1996), Myung et al. (2008) conducted research on restaurant attributes using conjoint analysis. However, there are important differences. The first study focused on preferences of different customer segments, but with a small sample size and a narrow number of attributes; its prediction power is very limited indeed. On the other hand, it used traditional conjoint analysis, which appears to be less natural to respondents than DCA. The second study, although it used DCA, was restricted to pizza restaurants, with fewer attributes in a limited sample of restaurants and a small sample size. The third piece of research used DCA as well but just concentrated on set menus.

On the other hand, it can also be noticed that although many recent studies have used DCA, a few still use traditional conjoint techniques with older studies such as the one of Wind et al. (1989) being very influential for further use of conjoint analysis in commercial and academic research. Research for academic papers appears to have limited resources because of the reliance on small sample sizes and use of respondents who may raise questions about representativeness, such as the choice of university students in the sample of the study of Koo and Koo (2010). The author has found that the development of conjoint analysis can be largely attributed to the work of researchers of Sawtooth Software who have published working papers of outstanding quality and are supported by the main authors in the area of conjoint analysis.

Research Design

Preliminary Considerations

Indeed, the research attempts to find explanations for decisions made by consumers in certain circumstances. A positivist, explanatory research will be adopted, particularly when attempting to ascertain attribute importance in different contexts. These attributes were ascertained in a previous qualitative stage (via research and an investigation of the literature). This research design has already been used to elicit meal attributes, but with a different focus. Indeed, Ding et al. (2005) started with a qualitative stage to understand the key attributes of Chinese dinner specials, and interviewed ten undergraduate students to determine what were key attributes to them and also what they perceived as important to their peers.

Discrete Choice Experiments

It seems more natural for consumers to make choices, not to rate or rank them (like in traditional conjoint analysis). Furthermore, as stated above, the use of technology has made that task more achievable. These advantages probably explain why DCA has become the natural choice for decision-making researchers using conjoint analysis methods. In DCA, the research design takes the form of DCEs. For instance, the decision maker responds to experimentally designed profiles of possible alternatives, in which each alternative has a different set of attributes (Verma and Thompson, 1996).

Sawtooth Software has developed Adaptive Choice-Based Conjoint (ACBC). ACBC is consistent with the theory that complex choices made by consumers entail the formation of a consideration set and then choosing a product within that consideration set (Orme, 2010).

Sampling Strategy

The study used a non-probability technique: respondent-driven sampling (RDS). Therefore unlike traditional probabilistic sampling in which it all starts with a sampling frame, RDS results in creating a sampling frame after sampling is complete (Wejnert and Heckathorn, 2008). Lately, the term of respondent-driven sampling (RDS) is used as a variation of the chain-referral sampling methods (Salganik and Heckathorn, 2004). The possibility of accessing large segments of respondents is a known fact as in populations as large as the United States, every person is indirectly associated with every other person through six waves (Killworth and Bernard, 1978).

Although the sampling strategy is considered to be non-probabilistic, it can be argued that due to the effect discussed by the six-degrees of separation theory (Milgram, 1964), magnified in the digital age (Kleinfeld, 2002), almost every respondent of the sampling frame can be randomly contacted through referent sampling. Formulas to establish optimum sample size require random samples; thus to estimate a sample size for this research, the sample will be assumed to be obtained at random, as for the considerations about the characteristics of the population above mentioned. For all these reasons, it is considered that the estimation formula that Louviere et al. (2000) provided for calculating optimum sample size for random samples is appropriate in this research:

$$N > \frac{qz^2}{rpa^2}.$$

In Louviere et al.'s formula, N represents the minimum number of participants; 'r' is the total number of choice scenarios or replications; 'p' is the choice share of a restaurant concept, $q = 1 - p$; 'z' is the confidence level under normal distribution; and 'a' is the allowable margin of error. In the choice tournaments, respondents will be shown three restaurant concepts with ten attributes showing a particular level; in this case, there are (3×10) 30 choice scenarios, $z = 1.96$ for a confidence level of 95%. If there are three choices, the probability of choices one is $1/3 = 0.33$, which is p. Then $q = 1 - 0.33 = 0.67$. If the margin of error is set at 5%, then:

$$N > \frac{0.67 \times (1.96)^2}{30 \times 0.33 \times (0.05)^2} = 104.$$

Therefore, according to this formula, the minimum sample size is 104 respondents for the ACBC sample. However, it is to be noted that this formula was derived for a simple selection, and in this case, several screens are showing several combinations of 30 choice scenarios. This added complexity for an accurate calculation of the sample size and the application of the formula. And in the case of large populations like the one in this research, Orme (2014) discussed that sample sizes for conjoint studies range from about 150 to 1,200 respondents. However, for ACBC, it has been found that in smaller sample sizes, ACBC would yield similar group-level errors, with 38% fewer participants than in traditional DCEs, such as the ones in CBC (Chapman et al., 2009). It also appears that smaller sample sizes compensate for the additional time required to complete ACBC surveys (Cunningham et al., 2010). As a minimum of 150 respondents is indicated as a rule of thumb and Louviere et al.'s formula points to a minimum of 104, the research attempted to get as many respondents as possible but not fewer than 150.

On the other hand, the first part of the research dealt with establishing which attributes are more important for certain segments, that is, which attributes are more relevant for this particular occasion or a particular age group, etc. In this case, we may consider the population to be very varied about a particular issue, for example, how many considered a particular attribute and how many would not? The maximum split, to be conservative, is a 50/50 split and has a sample size of 384; for a less varied population 80/20, the minimum number is 246. This is the sample aimed at the research.

Recruitment of Participants, Pilot Study and Final Sample

The first respondents were recruited through the professional network LinkedIn. The criteria for qualifying respondents were as follows:

a. The respondent should eat out at restaurants in the United Kingdom. In total, 6 out of 376 answered never (1.6%).

b. The respondent should be involved in making the decision. In total, 7 out of 376 answered never (1.9%).

c. To be of 19 years of age or above. In total, 6 out of 376 did not qualify (1.6%).

The final number (363) is well above the minimum requirement of 246 respondents and closer to the upper requirement level of 384 participants mentioned above. Although the ACBC module can work with up to 100 attributes, respondents can't choose efficiently with such a long list of attributes. Typical studies in practice cover about 5–12 attributes as recommended by Sawtooth Software. Prior to the choice tasks, a preliminary exercise of attribute reduction was conducted. Respondents had to choose from a total of 14 attributes – of which 5 are fixed. From the other 9 attributes, respondents had to choose 5. These 5 attributes will be called 'optional' attributes. Then there are 5 fixed attributes and 5 'optional attributes'. Therefore, 10 is the final number of attributes that any respondent would have to choose from during the choice tasks (choice tournament). The approach to pricing is summed pricing in which price is treated as a continuous variable. This means that pricing is affected by the choice of other attributes. Using the 'summed' pricing approach leads to restaurant concepts that show realistic prices. Restaurant with high-end features carry higher prices, and restaurants with low-end features carry lower prices. Under summed pricing, thousands of potential unique prices could be shown to respondents. The BYO section details more on how this works.

The Research Instrument

There are four main parts in the ACBC questionnaire, namely, the general information part (SSI web module of Sawtooth Software), Build Your Own, Screening section and Choice Tournament. The general part has demographic questions, the respondent chooses an occasion for eating out and also chooses the 'optional attributes' discussed above.

Figure 4.1 shows the BYO task, noting that there are nine attributes and that the higher the level, the greater the cost incurred. Adding all the individual costs per feature resulted in a total for the meal cost for one person.

Screening Section

In the screening section, four restaurant concepts are shown, for example, a restaurant that provides a particular level of service, with a level of variety, etc., and that concept also has a price tag. Some options like a greater level of service are more expensive. They are shown in Figure 4.2 in sequence order and preference order. Some options like ambiance have no preference order, meaning that whether they want a quiet or busy environment there is no record of the price paid.

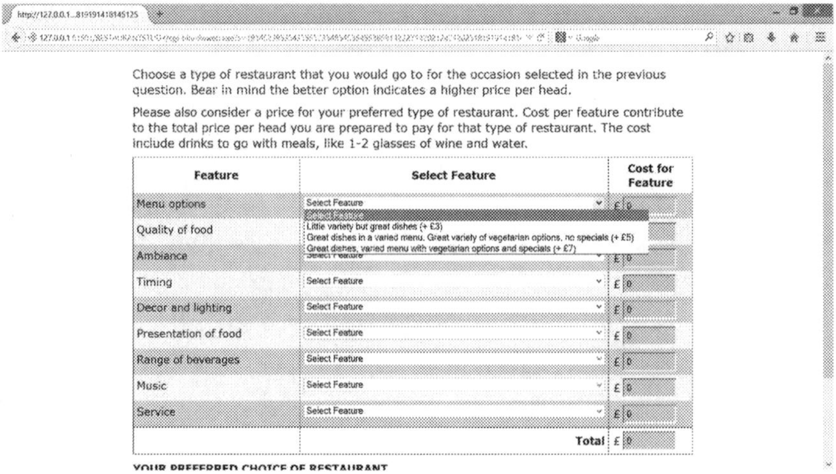

Figure 4.1   Features and cost per feature.

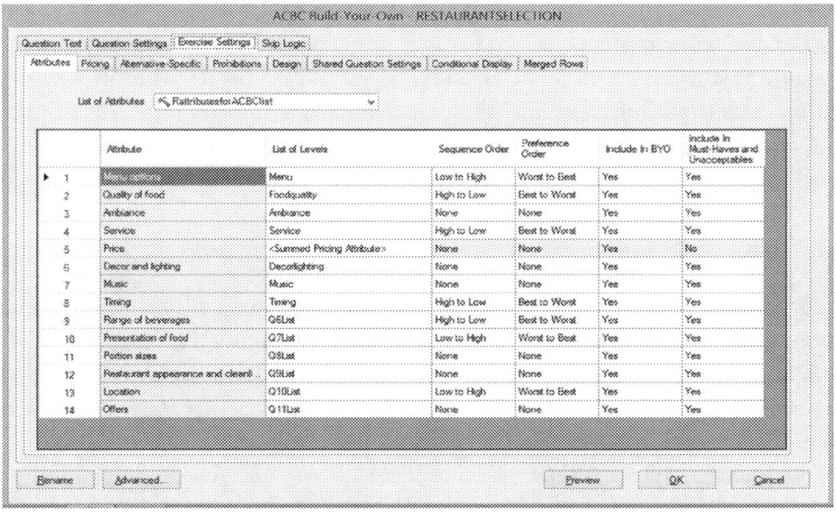

Figure 4.2   Total list of attributes with sequence and preference orders.

Choice Tournament

In the choice tournament section, the respondent was shown three restaurant concepts in each screen that survived the previous section. Eight choice tasks are shown, and respondents can choose only one of the concepts in each screen. An example can be seen in Figure 4.3.

The greyed-out rows show attributes that are tied across restaurant concepts so that respondents focus only on the remaining differences. Each choice results in a

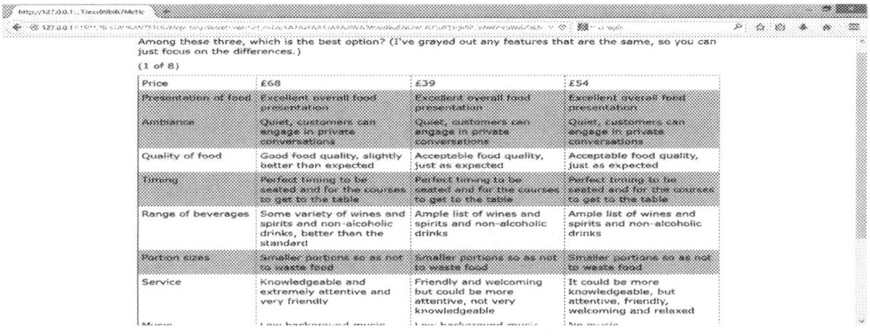

Among these three, which is the best option? (I've grayed out any features that are the same, so you can just focus on the differences.)

(1 of 8)

Price	£68	£39	£54
Presentation of food	Excellent overall food presentation	Excellent overall food presentation	Excellent overall food presentation
Ambiance	Quiet, customers can engage in private conversations	Quiet, customers can engage in private conversations	Quiet, customers can engage in private conversations
Quality of food	Good food quality, slightly better than expected	Acceptable food quality, just as expected	Acceptable food quality, just as expected
Timing	Perfect timing to be seated and for the courses to get to the table	Perfect timing to be seated and for the courses to get to the table	Perfect timing to be seated and for the courses to get to the table
Range of beverages	Some variety of wines and spirits and non-alcoholic drinks, better than the standard	Ample list of wines and spirits and non-alcoholic drinks	Ample list of wines and spirits and non-alcoholic drinks
Portion sizes	Smaller portions so as not to waste food	Smaller portions so as not to waste food	Smaller portions so as not to waste food
Service	Knowledgeable and extremely attentive and very friendly	Friendly and welcoming but could be more attentive, not very knowledgeable	It could be more knowledgeable, but attentive, friendly, welcoming and relaxed

Figure 4.3 Example of choice task.

winning concept that will then compete in subsequent rounds until the preferred concept is identified. That allows for understanding what attributes are the most important as they are trading them off with price.

Counting Analysis for ACBC

Counts can then be a good starting point for the analysis. However, if there is disagreement about which levels are preferred, then summaries of importance from aggregate counts can artificially bias estimates of attributes' importance. Therefore, a more accurate analysis of attribute importances can be determined using the utility values generated by hierarchical Bayes (HB) analysis.

HB Analysis: Calculation of Utilities and Importances

A utility is a number that represents the attractiveness of a feature, for example, 'great variety of dishes including vegetarian options and specials', which is one of the three levels for the attribute menu options. A basic problem has been to create individual-level utilities for each respondent (Howell, 2009). It should be noted that individual utilities offer more valuable information than looking into the average of a sample. For example, if there are two options concerning portion sizes and half of the respondents go for larger portions and the other half for smaller portions, the averaged result would conclude that consumers are ambivalent with regard to portion sizes and that can be the worst conclusion. With individual-level utilities, it is possible to distinguish market segments that go for larger portions and target them separately. In the ACBC exercise, the respondents have a screening section of ten choice tasks. If respondents select the attributes with the larger number of attributes, the maximum number of combinations is (5×4×2×4×4×5×4×3×5 = 192,000 combinations). It may seem an impossible task to estimate the preferences for that colossal number of combinations from the relatively small amount of information collected. The BYO and screening sections allow for a reduction in that number and then the choice tasks present (three restaurant concepts within the ten attributes, that is, 30 combinations at a time). Anyway estimating preferences accurately is a challenging task that can be done using HB analysis in the ACBC Sawtooth Software platform. HB is a useful tool for modeling consumer research phenomena (Rossi et al., 2005). About how well the solution (average utility part-worth of every respondent) fits the data, the value called root likelihood (RLH) offered an estimate. The best possible value is 1.00 and the worst possible is the inverse of the number of choices available in the average task; in this case, there are three choices, and thus that value is $(1/3 = 0.33)$. In some spread sheets, the system multiplies RLH by 1,000 so the worst possible value is 333 and the perfect fit is 1,000. The value of RLH obtained was 0.67 (670). It can be interpreted as just better than twice the chance level.

In conjoint studies, attribute importance can be derived from utility scores. The software determines importance scores by calculating the utility score range multiplied by 100%. The analysis looked into the difference in utility part-worths between levels of an attribute and the relative importance that each attribute will have for certain occasions.

HB with Covariates

Orme and Howell (2009) explained that when segmentation studies are conducted, distances between utility means of segments are diminished. This is because HB shrinks the individual estimates of the part-worths towards the population mean. It is better to ascertain whether there are significant differences between segments if that is possible. That can be done if HB with covariates is used rather than generic HB. This research needs to find out whether average importances differ according to the occasion of eating out and whether differences between levels of attributes are significantly different. Orme and Howell (2009) compared average importances for three segments with a generic HB run and with a covariates HB run, and found that there was almost 50% more spread in the latter for a particular attribute. This enhanced spread was not obtained by chance but because it offers a truer representation of their segment means because of a more accurate representation of population means in the HB upper model. This means that there is a more meaningful, robust and accurate analysis between segments. For that reason, HB with covariates will be conducted for looking at possible differences between occasions for eating out.

Results and Discussion

An Outline of the Different Tasks (Sections)

In the first section, the respondent built the original profile of their ideal restaurant; that is why it is called 'Build your Own'. The screening section entailed a trade-off exercise in which the respondent established attributes which are deemed as non-compensatory. Non-compensatory attributes are those for which a decrease in price will not compensate for a low level of the attribute, that is, a very low level of service (poor service). After the screening section, a reduced number of options were available to the respondent and after a series of tasks, a winning choice resulted. These sections contain counts and cross-tabulations with percentages.

This section concludes with the HB analysis. This analysis revealed differences between one level of an attribute and another level of an attribute. For example, if little variety is option 1, medium is 2 and high is 3, the difference between the part-worth given to option 2 is much greater than 1 but not that different from 3; this means that option 1 is not acceptable and that medium variety is the lowest he would accept. Therefore, the restaurateur would not have to spend so much effort in providing a variety of level 3 because that does not make much of a difference. Hence, HB analysis explicitly accounts for the differences in consumers' preferences by estimating individual part-worths.

Fixed Attributes

Acceptable food quality, just as expected, had almost the same preference as the next level (good food quality, slightly better than expected (34.5% v. 33%)). The highest level (Michelin-star or equivalent) was less preferred overall (26%). That level was preferred when the occasion was a romantic dinner. For menu options, the preferred level was the intermediate level of variety without specials (39.5% v. 33%). The greatest variety was preferred if the occasion was a birthday party or a special celebration. That may be because consumers assume the greater the variety, the more it can cater to the more varied tastes of a greater number of people on that occasion. All the same, the preference for little variety but greater dishes is significantly high (27.16%). This possibly means that there is a significant market segment of consumers who do not mind a shorter list of items on the menu if the quality is right. The winning concept exercise found that after several screens, service appears to grow in importance in this section when compared to the BYO section and the highest level of service (knowledgeable and extremely attentive and very friendly) has 40% preference compared to 29% and 18% for the next levels. This means that one segment of consumers is very appreciative of a higher level of service even if they have to pay more for it. This contrasts with the findings of BYO whereby 32% preferred the highest level. This means that a good number of consumers are willing to pay more for better service. In terms of ambiance, consumers prefer a quieter ambiance (65% v. 35%); in this case, it can be noted that parties may have a higher acceptance for busy places as also found in the BYO section.

Optional Attributes

The most selected attribute in this section was 'Restaurant cleanliness and appearance' with 233 completes. The findings confirmed what was found in the BYO section, about attractive furniture and tableware, which is preferred to innovative appearance (44% v. 29%). The preference for a clean but unpretentious restaurant as evidenced by 27% is almost the same as in the BYO section (29%). This result is revealing as many restaurateurs are spending large sums of money on unique designs, when basic attention to smaller details in décor, furniture and tableware are what consumers seem to be looking for. In this case, the choice of a quirky, innovative appearance did not mean a higher price, and even so this option was not highly favoured by respondents in the study.

Second in number of selections was location (210 completes). This section confirmed that having the choice of either parking facilities or public transport connections, parking facilities appear to be more important. In this case, 37% of respondents in the study preferred parking facilities to 25% who chose public transport connections. Likewise, a significant number (27%) were willing to pay more for a restaurant that has both features. It also confirmed that respondents in the study were not willing to accept going to restaurants with restricted accessibility as only 11% went for this option regardless of it being less costly.

Thirdly rated in order of completes was food presentation (199). As expected, non-compensatory behaviour was noticed as only 7% of respondents in the study went for 'presentation that needs some improvement', regardless of its lower cost. The winning choice was 'Good, slightly better than expected although unpretentious' (32%), which is the intermediate level. The next higher two levels excellent or outstanding were chosen by 23% and 21%. This means that for the respondents who chose presentation to be included as an optional attribute, there is some spread and further information is needed from the HB analysis of utility scores.

The fourth attribute in order of completes was décor and lighting (175). In this case, there was significant dispersion as 48% went for low lights compared to 52% for mid- to well-lit. A slightly higher preference was noticed for innovative décor (57%) compared to conservative décor (43%). Once more, the HB analysis of utility scores can be more enlightening.

The next attribute in order of completes was offers (101). As expected, if consumers included this aspect in this section, a low number was expected to go for no offers or sales incentives (13%). Here the preference for 'free items, money-off coupons, e-coupons' (36%) appears to be almost as high as 'Attractive pricing' (set menus, children menus, drinks included, etc.) with 34%. The least selected attributes in the number of completes were portion sizes (98), timing (88) and range of beverages (66).

Average Importances

The most important attribute, confirmed by other researchers in the literature review and the ACBC counts, was quality of food with 15.64%; second in importance was service with 11.16%. Atmospherics, as discussed in the literature review, is a complex issue that was further divided into other attributes such as a noisy or quiet ambiance (5.17%), décor and lighting (3.25%) and music (1.48%). If all these aspects are added together, this aspect showed an importance of 9.91%. Location seemed to be another important attribute with 6.92%, followed closely by food presentation that had an average importance of 5.74%. Interestingly, the attribute of menu options, included as a fixed attribute in the study, only measured an importance of 3.58%, which was close to the attribute of restaurant appearance and cleanliness (3.43%). Appearance was combined with cleanliness as a low level of cleanliness would not be accepted by respondents in the study as shown in the literature. But even when the features of appearance (unpretentious, innovative or quirky) were included, the importance of this attribute did not seem to increase. Interestingly, although a large percentage of respondents in the study decided to include it in the second part (over 90% for all occasions), the importance was considerably minimised when considered as a trade-off attribute in the second part of the survey (ACBC task). It seems that respondents in the study considered that it was an important attribute that restaurants must have but one that has less weight when other attributes have to be traded-off. The latter confirms the findings of Titz et al. (2004) who found that cleanliness was important only when not present. Thus, it is not generally part of the considerations when selecting a restaurant. Timing was even considered more important (4.60%). Aspects such as portion sizes and offers had low relative importance, 2.04% and 2.09%, respectively. Finally, the least important attribute was 'range of beverages' with 1.39%.

Interestingly, for food presentation, the highest utility was found for the highest level (19.15) but not markedly distant from the following levels, 15.31 and 16.58; however, it dropped significantly for the next level (acceptable presentation, almost as expected). This means that a certain 'Wow factor' is necessary when consumers listen to references about food presentation in a particular restaurant, if this is to be an influencing factor in the decision.

HB Analysis with Covariates

In this case, birthday parties and promotions were analysed as one occasion. Table 4.1 shows a comparison of average importances per occasion.

As for the most important attributes evaluated above, a significant difference was noticed in the importance of quality of food for a romantic dinner compared with quality for a night out or a celebration (19.42 compared to 14.89). That means that the couple going for a romantic dinner are willing to pay more for the highest quality, whilst they are not concerned about timing (3.79 compared to 5.36 for a celebration or a night out). This means that timing is of the utmost importance for restaurants organising parties as it is an important consideration in consumers' minds. Offers are of more importance for a normal night out with friends and family, with slightly less importance for celebrations but far less important for a romantic dinner occasion (0.97). Location seems to be more important for a night out with friends and family as well (7.49 compared to 6.52 for a romantic dinner and 5.12 for a special celebration). This may be because for a normal night out

Table 4.1   Average Importance per Occasion after HB Analysis with Covariates (N = 243)

Average Importances	Night Out	Romantic Dinner	Celebration
Menu options	3.46	3.87	3.74
Quality of food	14.89	19.42	14.89
Ambiance	5.08	5.20	4.71
Service	11.00	11.61	10.76
Décor and lighting	3.19	3.52	4.18
Music	1.07	2.48	2.26
Timing	4.72	3.79	5.36
Range of beverages	1.28	1.61	1.61
Presentation of food	5.74	5.71	5.29
Portion sizes	1.99	2.48	2.41
Restaurant appearance and cleanliness	3.41	3.12	4.82
Location	7.49	6.52	5.12
Offers	2.31	0.97	1.84

a convenient location with accessibility for different types of people is crucially important for selecting a restaurant. The aspect of restaurant appearance and cleanliness appeared to be more important for celebrations, as well as décor and lighting and music.

Difference in Levels of Attributes for Every Occasion

This section discusses every attribute. In some cases, the number of respondents in the study who chose to answer a particular attribute was particularly low. That is highlighted. Table 4.2 shows the differences between levels for menu options.

It can be noticed that greater variety was preferred if the occasion was a romantic dinner (14.90 compared to 7.39 for the next level). If the occasion is a party, greater variety was also important (13.50 compared to 4.73 for the next level). This confirms the findings in the counts of the winning concept. Table 4.3 shows the analysis of food quality and occasion.

In this case, the examination by occasion provides much more insightful information than the one obtained by counting. It confirms that if the occasion is a

Table 4.2 Utility Part-Worth for Menu Options after HB Analysis with Covariates (N = 243)

Menu Options	Night Out	Romantic Dinner	Celebration
Little variety but great dishes	−13.06	−22.29	4.73
Great dishes on a varied menu. Great variety of vegetarian options, no specials	6.48	7.39	4.73
Great dishes, varied menu with vegetarian options and specials	6.59	14.90	13.50

Table 4.3 Utility Part-Worth for Quality of Food after HB Analysis with Covariates (N = 243)

Quality of Food	Night Out	Romantic Dinner	Celebration
Excellent quality, worthy of awards (Michelin-star standard or close to it), very impressed.	51.07	91.99	72.06
Good food quality, slightly better than expected	54.83	79.73	37.18
Acceptable food quality, just as expected	18.39	−6.47	4.97
Slightly less than acceptable, needs some minor improvements	−124.29	−165.27	−114.23

romantic dinner, the utility is the greatest for the highest level; however, the difference between the highest level and the second-highest is greater if the occasion is a celebration, which shows a difference of about 35.00 (72.06–37.18). For romantic dinner, the difference is about 12.00 (91.99–79.73). Acceptable food quality had a much greater rate of acceptance (18.39) compared to romantic dinner (−6.47) or celebration (4.97) if the occasion was a normal day out with friends. Again, non-compensatory behaviour was observed across all segments as food of a sub-standard quality evidenced a remarkably low utility.

Table 4.4 shows the attribute of service per occasion for eating out.

Differences were not remarkable for the first two levels, and this means that customers were not prepared to pay much more for best quality of service. Interestingly, customers attending a party needed a type of service that is very attentive. This is shown in the table, as less knowledgeable service showed a utility of 3.94 compared

Table 4.4   Utility Part-Worth for Service after HB Analysis with Covariates (N = 243)

Service	Night Out	Romantic Dinner	Celebration
Knowledgeable and extremely attentive and very friendly	58.25	61.31	57.26
It could be more knowledgeable, but attentive, friendly, welcoming and relaxed	41.54	49.53	41.03
Friendly and welcoming but could be more attentive, not very knowledgeable	16.79	12.19	3.94
Attentive but a bit obtrusive and not particularly friendly or welcoming	−60.84	−81.77	−46.75
Relaxed and friendly, tries hard but leaves too much to be desired	−55.74	−55.49	−55.49

Table 4.5   Utility Part-Worth for Food Presentation after HB Analysis with Covariates (N = 243)

Food Presentation	Night Out	Romantic Dinner	Celebration
Presentation needs some improvement	−43.34	−30.45	−37.29
Acceptable presentation, almost as expected	−6.11	−25.05	−8.08
Good presentation, slightly better than expected although unpretentious	16.14	10.25	26.03
Excellent overall food presentation	16.61	16.17	12.49
Outstanding food presentation, beautiful and tempting	16.69	29.08	6.85

to 16.79 for a day/night out with friends and family and 12.19 for a romantic dinner. Service of poor quality had a remarkably low utility, which confirms non-compensatory behaviour. Table 4.5 showed the HB analysis with covariates of food presentation and occasion.

The HB analysis with covariates confirms that non-compensatory behaviour is evidenced because of the low utility for the lowest level. This analysis revealed that in the case of a romantic dinner, presentation is of great importance because of the

Table 4.6 Utility Part-Worth for Location after HB Analysis with Covariates (N = 243)

Location	Night Out	Romantic Dinner	Celebration
Public transport and parking not easily accessible	−56.31	−44.88	−32.12
Good parking facilities, public transport not easily accessible	9.81	9.70	19.23
Good public transport facilities, limited parking	11.79	24.29	6.18
Good parking and public transport connections	34.71	10.88	6.71

high utility for the highest level (29.08) compared to the next level (16.17), whereas for a night out with friends, there is almost no difference for the three highest levels and that for a celebration, good presentation, slightly better than expected, but unpretentious was preferred, which means that customers were prepared to pay more for other attributes but that presentation just has to be slightly better than expected. Overall food presentation was found to be important because 'acceptable presentation, almost as expected' showed low utility. Therefore, non-compensatory behaviour was observed for the lower levels. Table 4.6 looks into location and occasion.

Apart from the fact that poor accessibility had low utility for all occasions, the other levels presented notable differences. Customers were prepared to pay more for a well-located restaurant for a normal night out with friends and family. This may imply that when a night out with friends or family is planned, a convenient location for all attendees is needed. They may come by different means of transport. It may explain why it had the highest utility and it showed a considerable difference from the less convenient two levels below. However, for a romantic dinner when there are two eating out, public transport connections were preferred over parking. That means that they were prepared to pay more for other attributes like food presentation or food quality and service but not for the best located restaurant. In the case of celebrations, where preparations are made well in advance, highest utility is placed on a restaurant with good parking facilities (19.23), with less willingness to pay more for a well-located restaurant with both good parking facilities and public transport connections (6.71).

Conclusions

This research has conducted DCE for the very complex decision of selecting a restaurant. When more insight was needed, the HB analysis clarified what was not conclusive in the ACBC counts, adding more depth to the overall analysis of restaurant attributes. When trading off price, respondents are willing to accept food quality of acceptable or good quality so as to avoid the premium attached to award-winning restaurants. Higher levels were preferred if the occasion is a romantic dinner. The survey also revealed that a significant percentage of respondents favoured a quiet restaurant with higher acceptance of a slightly noisy atmosphere for birthday parties. Attractive furniture and tableware was preferred to innovative appearance, and clean but unpretentious restaurants are also appreciated to a high degree. Contrastingly, innovative décor was chosen more than conservative décor. Overall, the survey revealed that quirky, innovative design is not sought after. This is an interesting finding, particularly because this attribute was not linked to higher prices. It means that spending a great deal of money in design will not draw more customers but that spending that money on attractive furniture and tableware is wiser (and less costly). For this smaller sample, timing seems particularly relevant with 60% of respondents selecting the level of perfect timing as a feature of their preferred restaurant regardless of its higher price When occasion was considered, respondents were prepared to pay more for Michelin-star standard food quality for romantic dinners than for a night out with friends/family. It was found that menu variety is more important if the occasion is a party, in which case consumers are prepared to pay more. Location is another key attribute, and poor accessibility was not accepted. Parking was found to be more important than public transport connections for all occasions, except romantic dinners. This exercise also confirmed the paramount importance of parking facilities with low acceptance for restaurants with restricted accessibility regardless of their being less costly. Price-sensitive consumers were found to have the same preference for 'free items, money-off coupons, e-coupons' as for 'Attractive pricing (set menus, children's menus, drinks included, etc.)'. The highest level of food presentation, outstanding, is more highly selected for romantic dinners or a birthday party and significantly less for the occasion of day/night out with friends and families. For menu options, the preferred level was the intermediate level of variety without specials and the higher level of variety was preferred if the occasion is a party. It seems that party goers expect food of great variety to cater for different tastes. Nonetheless, the preference for 'little variety but greater dishes' is significantly high. This may mean that quality supersedes variety. Respecting service, it was found that as the survey progressed, in the last tasks (after further reasoning and trading-off attributes) the significance of higher levels of service increases. For instance, the highest level of service (knowledgeable and extremely attentive and very friendly) had the highest (40%) preference compared to the lower levels. This means that a good number of consumers are willing to pay more for better service. As for the least selected options, respondents favour larger portions over smaller portions.

The survey confirmed non-compensatory behaviour in various attributes like food quality and service with low acceptance for lowest levels regardless of these having a lower price. Timing was another important attribute and a substantial percentage of all 'unacceptables' referred to having to wait for the courses or to be seated. This becomes then an aspect that restaurant managers must consider as critical. Location is another attribute that shows non-compensatory behaviour with an important number of respondents considering that location that has limited parking facilities or public transport connections is unacceptable. Presentation of food is deemed to be the other relevant element exhibiting non-compensatory behaviour because only a small percentage of respondents selected presentation that needed some improvement, regardless of its lower cost.

The HB analysis provided more detail about differences in preferences for attributes than the counts. The most important attribute, confirmed by other researchers in the literature review and in the interviews, was quality of food with 15.64%. Second in importance was service with 11.16%. Atmospherics, as combining ambiance (noisy or quiet), décor and lighting and music, showed an importance of 9.91%. Location followed with 6.92%, then food presentation with 5.74%. Menu options, although included as a fixed attribute in the study, only measured an importance of 3.58%, similar to restaurant appearance and cleanliness (3.43%).

The HB analysis looked at significant differences between levels in order to determine, for example, minimum levels of services that are required. Concerning food quality, it was found that customers are prepared to pay more for something that is better than expected, but it seems that the high price associated with top-end restaurants makes the difference between the restaurants with award-winning standards and the next lower level relatively small; therefore, for most customers having to pay more for the option of Michelin-star standards was rather unaffordable. The results about service confirmed what had been found in the counting analysis. The difference between the highest level, friendly, welcoming and knowledgeable (59.10) and the next level (42.26) is significant, but more significant is the difference from the next level (friendly and welcoming but could be more attentive, not very knowledgeable) with 15.07. It was found that there is a higher preference for relaxed and friendly service but is poor in terms of attentiveness and knowledge (−52.69) to an attentive service that is nonetheless obtrusive and not very friendly or welcoming (−63.74). Concerning location, the difference between the highest level – good parking and public transport connections – with 27.37 and the next level (good public transport facilities but limited parking) with 13.28 is significant. The next level (good public transport facilities and limited parking) had a very similar utility (11.18). It can be concluded that well-located restaurants have a higher likelihood to be selected than less-well located ones. In the case of food presentation, a certain 'Wow factor' is found to be important for a restaurant to be selected when considering this attribute. This is because the difference in utility between the second level (acceptable presentation, almost as expected) and the third level (good presentation, slightly better than expected) was found to be significant for all occasions. Innovative décor is highly preferred to conservative décor with a slight preference for mid- to well-lit.

Finally, the analysis of utilities confirmed that offers such as money off coupons and attractive pricing (bundles, etc.) have almost the same level of preference (4.90 v. 5.25). Perfect timing is confirmed to be significantly more preferred than the next level (29.72 v. 9.69). This seems to imply that timing is another key factor when considered.

Implications for the Restaurant Industry

The first implication for the restaurant industry is that a good way of segmenting restaurant consumers is by occasion for eating out and the survey revealed particular differences in these segments. It may mean that positioning restaurants should be based on targeting those consumers that look for restaurants which focus on the attributes and attribute levels for consumers who go to restaurants for particular occasions. The research has found that the required levels of attributes may vary according to the occasion. For example, when occasion was considered, respondents were prepared to pay more for Michelin-star standard food quality for romantic dinners than for a normal night out with friends/family. Generally, music was not highly sought after, with some acceptance for romantic dinners and celebrations. Restaurant appearance and cleanliness appeared to be more important for celebrations, as well as décor and lighting. Greater variety of menu options was preferred if the occasion was a romantic dinner or for parties. Timing was particularly important for parties as well. The research has shown that when investing in new restaurants, key to the decision is location, so a good location seems to be a vital factor for the decision to select the restaurant. In terms of food quality, it has been confirmed that the required threshold is food quality as expected. Customers have a high appreciation for service that is attentive, welcoming and friendly and are prepared to pay more for that service. Knowledgeable service appeared to less important than attentiveness and friendliness, although the preference for knowledgeable service cannot be dismissed. Also, friendliness is preferred over attentiveness, if attentiveness borders on intrusiveness. An important finding is that consumers are not looking for an innovative, quirky type of design. Even though some restaurateurs spend great amounts of money on décor, consumers do not find higher value in eccentric design. This is even stressed by the fact that in the survey consumers would not have to pay higher prices for innovative décor (which indeed could be the case), and still they preferred a more sober interior decoration and design. Also, it was found that having other aspects of the restaurant service right is much more important that providing offers and incentives to customers.

Reflections on Limitations of This Research

With regard to data collection methods, the use of the full profile approach in the online survey and the several tasks that respondents had to complete made the survey fairly long and the rate of incomplete surveys was perhaps too high. Of course, it was a compromise between having a shorter survey completed by a larger number of respondents with reduced insight, or alternatively a smaller sample with more detailed insight. The latter seems to have been proved to produce more discerning results. However, it has to be conceded that being able to reach to a larger population would have enhanced accuracy indicators, but there were resources constraints and restrictions on participant recruitment that made a larger sample difficult. On the other hand, respondents had to recall an occasion for selecting a restaurant, and there are problems when respondents are asked to recall. If possible, research could take the form of an experiential survey in which respondents are indeed answering questions about how they selected that particular restaurant for that particular experience. Of course, that will be more demanding and entails liaising with a restaurant business to make it possible plus the monetary problem of incentivising the respondents for increased participation in the survey. Further research should be made on particular occasions for selecting a restaurant and on an examination of other occasions, for example, business dining.

Despite its limitations, it is considered that several worthwhile contributions can be drawn from this research. First of all, it offers a methodological design for the use of DCA for the decision of selecting a restaurant. Finally, it delivers insights into the importance of restaurant attributes for several occasions with interesting implications for the restaurant industry.

References

Andaleeb, S. S., & Conway, C. (2006). Customer satisfaction in the restaurant industry: An examination of the transaction-specific model. *Journal of Services Marketing*, 20(1), 3–11.

Ben-Akiva, M., McFadden, D., Abe, M., et al. (1997). Modelling methods for discrete choice analysis. Marketing Letters, 8(3), 273–286.

Ben-Akiva, M., & Lerman, S. R. (1985). *Discrete Choice Analysis: Theory and Applications to Travel Demand*. Cambridge, MA: MIT Press.

Campbell-Smith, G. (1967). *The Marketing of the Meal Experience*. Guildford: University of Surrey Press.

Capstick, L. (ed) (2011). *Restaurants: Market Report Plus 2011*. Teddington: Key Note.

Chapman, C. N., Alford, J. L., Johnson, C., et al. (2009). CBC vs. ACBC: Comparing results with real product selection. In Sawtooth Software Inc., editors. *2009 Proceedings of Sawtooth Software Conference Proceedings*, USA, 199–206.

Charles, N., & Kerr, M. (1988). *Women, Food, and Families*. Manchester: Manchester University Press.

Cousins, J., Foskett, D., & Gillespie, C. (2002). *Food and Beverage Management*, 2nd edition. Harlow: Prentice Hall.

Cunningham, C. E., Deal, K., & Chen, Y. (2010). Adaptive choice-based conjoint analysis: A new patient-centred approach to the assessments of health service preferences. *Patient*, 3(4), 257–273.

Davis, F. D., & Warshaw, P. R. (1991). Choice sets and choice intentions. *The Journal of Social Psychology*, 131(6), 823–830.

Denstadli, J. M., & Lines, R. (2007). Conjoint respondents as adaptive decision makers. *International Journal of Market Research*, 49(1), 117–132.

Devetag, M. G. (1999). From utilities to mental models: A critical survey on decision rules and cognition in consumer choice. *Industrial and Corporate Change*, 8(2), 1–78.

Ding, M., Grewal, R., & Liechty, J. (2005). Incentive-aligned conjoint analysis. *Journal of Marketing Research*, 42(1), 67–82.

Dulen, J. (1999). Quality control. *Restaurant & Institutions*, 109(5), 38–52.

Gensch, D. H., & Soofi, E. S. (1995). Information-theoretic estimation of individual consideration set. *International Journal of Research in Marketing*, 12(1), 25–38.

Green, P. E., Krieger, A. M., & Wind, Y. (2001). Thirty years of conjoint analysis: Reflections and prospects. *Interfaces*, 31(3), 56–73.

Green, P. E., & Srinivasan, V. (1990). Conjoint analysis in marketing: New developments with implications for research and practice. *Journal of Marketing*, 54(4), 3–19.

Hargreaves-Heap, S., Hollis, M., Lyons, B., Sugden, R., & Weale, A. (1992). *The Theory of Choice – A Critical Guide*. Oxford: Blackwell.

Harrington, R. J., Ottenbacher, M. C., & Way, K. A. (2013). QSR choice: Key restaurant attributes and the roles of gender, age and dining frequency. *Journal of Quality Assurance in Hospitality & Tourism*, 14(1), 81–100.

Horowitz, J. L., & Louviere, J. L. (1995). What is the role of consideration sets in choice modelling? *International Journal of Research in Marketing*, 12(1), 39–54.

Howard, J. A. (1963). *Marketing Management: Analysis and Planning*. Homewood, IL: Richard D. Irwin.

Howell, J. (2009). *CBC/HB for Beginners*. Sawtooth Software Inc. http://www.sawtooth-software.com/download/techpap/CBCHBbeginners.pdf.

Hsee, C. K., & Tsai, C. I. (2008). Hedonomics in consumer behavior. In C. P. Haugtvedt, P. M. Herr, & F. R. Kardes (Eds.), *Marketing and Consumer Psychology Series: Vol. 4. Handbook of Consumer Psychology* (pp. 639–657). New York: Taylor & Francis Group/Lawrence Erlbaum Associates.

Jang, S., Liu, Y., & Namkung, Y. (2011). Effects of authentic atmospherics in ethnic restaurants: Investigating Chinese restaurants. *International Journal of Contemporary Hospitality Management*, 23(5), 662–680.

Killworth, P. D., & Bernard, H. R. (1978–1979). The reversal small world experiment. *Social Networks*, 1(2), 159–192.

Kim, W. G., Lee, Y. K., & Yoo, Y. J. (2006). Predictors of relationship quality and relationship outcomes in luxury restaurants. *Journal of Hospitality & Tourism Research*, 30(2), 143–169.

Kleinfeld, J. (2002 April). Could it be a big world after all? The six degrees of separation myth. *Society*, 12, 5–2.

Koo, H. Y. H., & Koo, L. C. (2010). Empirical examination of AHP and Conjoint Analysis on casino attributes in Macau. In *Conference Proceedings of an International Conference on Public Welfare and Gaming Industry*, Beijing 9–11 December, pp. 327–350.

Koo, L. C., Tao, F. K. C., & Yeung, J. H. C. (1999). Preferential segmentation of restaurant attributes through conjoint analysis. *International Journal of Contemporary Hospitality Management*, 11(5), 242–250.

Law, R., To, T., & Goh, C. (2008). How do Mainland Chinese travellers choose restaurants in Hong Kong? An exploratory study of individual visit scheme travellers and packaged travellers. *International Journal of Hospitality Management*, 27(3), 346–354.

Lincoln, N. K., Lynham, S. A., & Guba, E. G. (2011). Paradigmatic controversies, contradictions, and emerging confluences. In N. K. Denzin, & Y. S. Lincoln (Eds.), *The Sage Handbook of Qualitative Research* (4th edition, pp. 97–128). London: Sage.

Liu, Y., & Jang, S. S. (2009). Perceptions of Chinese restaurants in the US: What affects customer satisfaction and behavioural intentions? *International Journal of Hospitality Management*, 28(3), 338–348.

Louviere, J. J. (1988). *Analysing Decision Making*. London: Sage.

Louviere, J. J., Flynn, T. N., & Carson, R. C. (2010). Discrete choice experiments are not conjoint analysis. *Journal of Choice Modelling*, 3(3), 57–72.

Louviere, J. J., Hensher, D. A., & Swait, J. D. (2000). *Stated Choice Methods: Analysis and Application*. Cambridge: Cambridge University Press.

Macht, M., Meininger, J., & Roth, J. (2005). The pleasures of eating: A qualitative analysis. *Journal of Happiness Studies*, 6(2), 137–160.

Mamalis, S. (2009). Critical success factors of the foodservice industry. *Journal of International Food & Agribusiness Marketing*, 21(2–3), 191–206.

Mazzocchi, M. (2008). *Statistics for Marketing and Consumer Research*. London: Sage.

Mehta, S. S., & Maniam, B. (2002). Marketing determinants of customers' attitudes towards selecting a restaurant. *Academy of Marketing Studies Journal*, 6(1), 27–44.

Meng, J. G., & Elliott, K. M. (2008). Predictors of relationship quality for luxury restaurants. *Journal of Retailing and Consumer Services*, 15(6), 509–515.

Milgram, S. (1967). The small world problem. *Psychology Today*, 1(1), 61–67.

Mittal, V., Ross, W. T., & Baldasare, P. M. (1998). The asymmetric impact of negative and positive attribute-level performance on overall satisfaction and repurchase intentions. *Journal of Marketing*, 62(1), 33–47.

Myung, E., Feinstein, A. H., & McCool, A. C. (2008). Using a discrete choice model to identify consumer meal preferences within a prix fixe menu. *Journal of Hospitality & Tourism Research*, 32(4), 491–504.

Namkung, Y., & Jang, S. S. (2008). Are highly satisfied restaurant customers really different? A quality perception perspective. International Journal of Contemporary Hospitality Management, 20(2), 142–155.

Narayana, C. L., & Martin, R. J. (1975). Consumer behaviour and product performance: An alternative conceptualization. *Journal of Marketing*, 39(4), 1–6.

Narine, T., & Badrine, N. (2007). Influential factors affecting food choices of consumers when eating outside the household in Trinidad, West Indies. *Journal of Food Products Marketing*, 13(1), 19–29.

Orme, B., & Howell, J. (2009). *Application of Covariates within Sawtooth Software CBC/HB Programme: Theory and Practical Example*. Sequim, WA: Sawtooth Software Research Paper Series.

Orme, B. K (2010). *Getting Started with Conjoint Analysis: Strategies for Product Design and Pricing Research*, 2nd edition. Madison, WI: Research Publishers LLC.

Orme, B. K (2014). *Getting Started with Conjoint Analysis: Strategies for Product Design and Pricing Research*, 3rd edition. Madison, WI: Research Publishers LLC.

Pantelidis, I. S. (2010). Electronic meal experience: A content analysis of online restaurant comments. *Cornell Hospitality Quarterly*, 51(4), 483–491.

Ribeiro-Soriano, D. (2002). Customers' expectations factors in restaurants: The situation in Spain. *International Journal of Quality & Reliability Management*, 19(8/9), 1055–1067.

Roberts, J., & Nedungadi, P. (1995). Studying consideration in the consumer decision process: Progress and challenges. *International Journal of Marketing*, 12(1), 3–7.

Rossi, P., Allenby, G., & McCulloch, R. (2005). *Bayesian Statistics and Marketing*, Chichester: John Wiley & Sons.

Salganik, M. J., & Heckathorn, D. D. (2004). Sampling and estimation in hidden populations using respondent-driven sampling. *Sociological Methodology*, 34(1), 193–239.

Shah, A. K., & Oppenheimer, D. M. (2008). Heuristics made easy: An effort-reduction framework. *Psychological Bulletin*, 134(2), 207–222.

Shocker, A. D., Ben-Akiva, M., Boccara, B., & Nedungadi, P. (1991). Consideration set influences on consumer decision making and choice: Issues, models, and suggestions. *Marketing Letters*, 2(3), 181–197.

Simon, H. (1992). Decision making and problem solving. In M. Zey (Ed,), *Decision Making –Alternatives to Rational Choice Models*, pp. 32–53. London: Sage.

Solomon, M. R. (2007). *Consumer Behaviour*, 7th edition. Upper Saddle River, NJ: Mc Graw Hill.

Statt, D. A. (1997). *Understanding the Consumer: A Psychological Approach.* London: Palgrave.

Sukalakamala, P., & Boyce, J. B. (2007). Customer perceptions for expectations and acceptance of an authentic dining experience in Thai restaurants. Journal of Foodservice, 18(2), 69–75.

Susskind, A. M., & Chan, E. K. (2000). How restaurant features affect check averages: A study of the Toronto restaurant market. *Cornell Hotel and Restaurant Administration Quarterly*, 41(6), 56–63.

Titz, K., Lanza-Abbott, J. A., & Cruz, G. C. Y. (2004). The anatomy of restaurant reviews: An exploratory study. *International Journal of Hospitality & Tourism Administration*, 5(1), 49–65.

Verma, R., Plaschka, G., & Louviere, J. J. (2002). Understanding customer choices: A key to successful management of hospitality services. *Cornell Hospitality Quarterly*, 43(6), 15–24.

Verma, R., & Thompson, G. (1996). Basing service management on customer determinants. *Cornell Hospitality Quarterly*, 37(3), 18–23.

Victorino, L., Verma, R., Plaschka, G., & Dev, C. (2005). Service innovation and customer choices in the hospitality industry. *Managing Service Quality*, 15(6), 555–576.

Wall, E. A., & Berry, L. L. (2007). The combined effects of the physical environment and employee behaviour on customer perception of restaurant service quality. Cornell Hotel and Restaurant Administration Quarterly, 48(1), 59–69.

Walker, J. R. (2014). *Exploring the Hospitality Industry*, 2nd edition. Harlow: Pearson.

Wejnert, C., & Heckathorn, D. D. (2008). Web-based network sampling efficiency and efficacy of respondent-driven sampling for online research. *Sociological Methods Research*, 37(1), 105–134.

Wind, J., Green, P. E., Shifflet, D., & Scarborough, M. (1989). Courtyard by Marriott: Designing a hotel facility with consumer based marketing models. *Interfaces*, 19(1), 25–47.

Wood, R. C. (1994). Dining out on sociological neglect. *British Food Journal,* 96(10), 141–162.

Wright, P. (1975). Consumer choice strategies: Simplifying vs. optimizing. *Journal of Marketing Research*, 12(1), 60–67.

Chapter 5

Data Analytics in Marketing and Customer Analytics

Rajasekhara Mouly Potluri and Gerry N. Muuka

Al Ghurair University

Contents

Introduction

In today's highly competitive business world, all entrepreneurs and managers in every part of the globe, irrespective of the type and magnitude of the business, must make numerous decisions related to so many business issues. Among the most significant of these decisions are customer related and marketing related. This is so because the marketing department in any company is the frontline unit in matters of getting final goods and services to the consumer, thereby proving the revenues needed for organizations to not only survive, but to also grow and prosper. Mistakes related to any business decision in general and marketing decisions in particular—most notably those associated with the product, price, place, promotion, and customer related—could cost businesses heavily, going so far as to threaten the very survival of companies and organizations.

The marketing department and its think-tank must be vigilant with the utmost care and diligence to take any decisions related to either the four Ps (for physical products marketing) or the seven Ps (for services marketing) because of its significance in achieving the firm's short-term, medium-term, as well as long-term goals and objectives. Most businesses have the singular intention of making a profit even though they have some degree of socially responsible actions in their mind as part of their corporate social responsibility (CSR). Whatever decisions managers take in, business organizations have direct or tangential economic consequences. What makes their decisions and decision-making processes more difficult is the fact that critical information about the future—upon which such decisions are made—is at best imperfect. One need look no further than the global economy since March 2020 during the advent of the Corona virus pandemic. Not only are customers restricted to their homes in much of the world since March 2020—meaning that they cannot access most goods and services at the usual locations and points of sale—for most multinational corporations (MNCs) and transnational corporations (TNCs) it is difficult to impossible to get their global operations on track because world business and commerce has almost come to a standstill. Both air travel and sea travel—for human beings and commerce—have been hampered by a pandemic (the Corona virus) that has spared no nation on earth. Borders are closed in much of the world, meaning that commercial aircraft that normally carry millions of passengers into and out of airports everyday are simply parked and cannot fly. Sea travel is also limited, meaning that marine transportation of humans and goods is also severely curtailed. Under these unusual and unprecedented circumstances and conditions, even the best managers and decision-makers utilizing the best tools at their disposal cannot operate with any degree of certainty.

During more certain times—*absent the current conditions brought about by the Corona virus*—managers need upright and relevant data and backing to make crucial decisions that will impact not only their companies but also their careers. Most managers in the business world face a complicated situation because of an overwhelming amount of available data and information. With this massive amount of data available from various primary and secondary sources along with web-based sources, managers are in a pandemonium situation to find out the most appropriate and trustworthy data, which is more applicable to the existing decision-making activity. Data to support business decisions, including those exclusively accumulated by firms from all kinds of sources, are increasing exponentially and becoming challenging to understand and utilize and are the critical reason why data analytics is vital in today's business environment.

Chapter Objectives and Learning Outcomes

This chapter provides a general introduction about the importance of data in managerial decision-making, including the definitions of core concepts viz., data analytics, business analytics, marketing and marketing management, customer and consumer, along with the significance of marketing and customer analytics. This chapter describes the marketing management process, which consists of critical stages such as research, segmentation, targeting, and positioning (STP), designing the marketing mix, marketing implementation, and control and analytics importance at every stage of marketing management. At the close of this chapter, the authors discuss the managerial implications of this important chapter, along with some key conclusions.

At the conclusion of this chapter, the reader will be able to understand the underlying conceptual knowledge on data analytics, business analytics, marketing and marketing management, customers and consumers, along with why analytics is vital in today's highly volatile business environment. Students can also learn different steps in the marketing management process and the role of analytics at every stage of management of marketing. Students will have exposure to information about customer analytics and the three types of decision-makers in any organization where customer analytics is applied as a practical and pragmatic concept.

Definitions of Data Analytics, Business Analytics, Marketing and Marketing Management, Marketing Analytics, Customers and Consumers, Customer Analytics

Data Analytics

Data analytics is the science of examining the raw data with the application of several statistical tools and techniques to make conclusions about the information with multiple data-driven decisions and insights. It is applicable in almost all industries to allow organizations and companies to make improved decisions as well as substantiate and challenge prevailing concepts or patterns. The emphasis of data analytics remains an implication, which is the process of obtaining conclusions that are exclusively established on what the researcher already identifies. The techniques and procedures of data analytics have been automated into mechanical processes and algorithms that work over raw data for human consumption with the help of machine learning and artificial intelligence. Data analytics optimizes business performance to the maximum level by reducing the costs and increasing profitability through sales.

According to Runkler (2012), data analytics is defined as "the application of computer system to the analysis of large data sets for the backing of decisions." Runkler (2012) goes on to explain that data analytics is necessarily an interdisciplinary field that borrows heavily from such different fields and subjects as statistics, signal theory, pattern recognition, computational intelligence, machine learning, and operations research.

Business Analytics

Business analytics, also simply referred to as analytics, is the usage of data, information technology (IT), statistical analysis, quantitative methods, as well as mathematical and computer-based models to help managers to obtain an understanding about their business operations to make improved reality-based decisions. Different authors have defined the concept of business analytics differently. Those presented below are by no means exhaustive:

The simplest explanation is given by Laursen and Thorlund (2016) in their book *Business Analytics for Managers: Taking Business Intelligence beyond Reporting*. They conceptualize business analytics as "delivering the right decision support to the right people at the right time."

Liberatore and Luo (2010) view business analytics as "a process of transforming data into actions through analysis and insights in the context of organizational decision making and problem-solving."

Marketing and Marketing Management

Marketing is all about winning the hearts of markets by identifying and meeting human and social needs. The Marketing Guru and Father of Modern Marketing, the American Professor Philip Kotler gave the shortest and most straightforward definition of marketing as "meeting needs profitably." Along with his associates, Prof. Kotler distinguishes between a social and a managerial definition of marketing. They gave the social angle of the marketing as to mean "delivering a higher standard of living" and the managerial perspective of marketing as "the art of selling products." The Management Guru, another American, Peter F. Drucker (1973) said that marketing aims to make selling superfluous or unnecessary and to know and understand the customer so well that the product or service fits him and sells itself.

Kotler and Armstrong (2016) defined marketing as "the process by which companies create value for customers and build strong customer relationships in order to capture value from customers in return."

As per the 2017 reapproved definition provided by the American Marketing Association (AMA, 2017a), "Marketing is the activity, set of institutions, and processes for creating, communicating, delivering, and exchanging offerings that have value for customers, clients, partners, and society at large." Marketing management therefore involves planning, implementation, and control of all the marketing activities in an organization to design strategies that will engage target customers and build profitable, long-lasting relationships with them.

Kotler and Keller (2018) defined marketing management as "the art and science of choosing target markets and getting, keeping, and growing customers through creating, delivering, and communicating superior customer value."

Kotler and Armstrong (2016) defined marketing management as "the art and science of choosing target markets and building profitable relationships with them."

Customer and Consumer

These two words, namely, customer and consumer, are some of the most widely and confusingly used concepts in the business world even though a crystal-clear difference exists between them. Generally, the customer is an individual, institution, or organization who is buying goods and services for another sale. In contrast, consumers are people, institutions, or organizations that purchase products and services for their consumption. However, in common parlance, most business organizations in fact use these two terms and concepts interchangeably.

Depending on the firm's business, a *customer* is defined as "an individual, household, screen-name, division, or business who bought, ordered, or registered" (Farris et al., 2010). The American Marketing Association (2014) defines "customer" as "the actual or prospective purchaser of products or services."

Conventionally, a *consumer* is the ultimate user or consumer of goods, ideas, and services. However, the term is also used to imply the buyer or *decision-maker* as well as the *final consumer*. Such is the case when a mother buys cereal for consumption by a small child called the consumer, although the mother is not the ultimate user (American Marketing Association, 2014).

Marketing Analytics and Its Significance

Marketing analytics is the preparation for measuring, managing, and analyzing marketing performance to maximize its effectiveness and optimize return on investment (ROI). *Marketing analytics* involves the discovery and communication of meaningful patterns in data from metrics like traffic, leads, sales, advertising, promotions, web activity, social media, and any other relevant marketing activity or financial data. According to the Common Language in Marketing Project (2016), marketing analytics

> can be defined by their use of mathematical distributions, statistical sources, or analytical techniques (e.g., regression) for their construction. These analytical techniques may represent the causal relationships among various conditions and actions taken to achieve specific business results, and are often used to inform future marketing actions.

Marketing analytics includes the practices and know-hows that facilitate marketers to assess the accomplishment of their marketing programs. Marketing analytics manages critical business metrics, such as ROI, marketing attribution, and overall marketing effectiveness. In other words, it tells the company about how the company's marketing programs are performing. Marketing analytics permit the marketer to examine operations and their corresponding results, facilitating marketing think-tanks to spend each dollar as effectively as feasible. The significance of marketing analytics is apparent: if something costs more than it returns, it is not a decent long-term business strategy. It considers all marketing efforts across all channels over time, which is vital for sound decision-making and competent, efficient program execution. Further, along with crucial sales, remaining lead marketing operations, marketing analytics can peel into a deeper understanding of customer-first choices and developments. Despite these fascinating advantages, many organizations—especially in the developing world—fail to realize the promises of marketing analytics. The problem is less severe in professionally managed organizations in the developed world.

Customer Analytics and Its Role

Customer analytics is a process by which data from customer behavior is used to help make critical business decisions via market segmentation and predictive analytics. Businesses use this information for direct marketing, site selection, and customer relationship management (CRM). Marketing provides different kinds of services to enhance customer satisfaction. Customer analytics portrays an essential role in the prediction of customer behavior (Kioumarsi et al., 2009). The SAS (2020) website gave a comprehensive definition, asserting that customer analytics "refers to the processes and technologies that give organizations the customer insight necessary to deliver offers that are anticipated, relevant and timely (https://www.sas.com/en_ae/insights/marketing/customer-analytics.html)." SAS (2020) goes on to point out that core function of customer relationship management is to organize the collection and use of customer information under customer analytics. Authors such as Lichtenstein, David, and Stewart (2008) defined customer analytics as "that part of the CRM system that involves the systematic collection, warehousing, analysis and deployment of customer data."

In contemporary business, customers are exposed to the vast quantity of data from different sources to decide on their buying, particularly what, when, where, how to buy, and how much to pay. In these circumstances, it is increasingly necessary for all marketers to acquire a thorough customer insight to understand how their target market customers will behave when interacting with the organization. The deeper the marketers' understanding of their customers' buying motives, spending patterns, and lifestyle preferences, the more precise predictions of future buying behaviors will be vital for their success. The core focus of customer analytics is on understanding and modeling customers' past behavior and predicting their future behavior. This includes elements of CRM, Business Intelligence, and Marketing Insights (MI). Customer analytics leads to better, informed, and data-driven decisions. It connects a variety of data points and sets to recognize and categorize trends, patterns, anomalies, and gaps.

The Marketing Management Tasks and Process

Tasks of Marketing Management

Managing the marketing function is not an easy task because of a confluence of factors including, but not limited to, severe competition, the highly volatile nature of both macro- and microenvironmental elements, changing trends of consumer preferences, and lately of course, the unprecedented negative global impact of the Corona virus pandemic on the entire fabric of business and human life. Keep in mind, the objective of any company and goal of the marketing department is to engage in a series of tasks to win the hearts of the market/customers/consumers.

According to Kotler and Keller (2016), there is set of primary responsibilities necessary for successful marketing management. The responsibilities include, but are not limited to, the following:

a. Developing marketing strategies and plans
b. Capturing marketing insights
c. Connecting with customers
d. Building strong brands
e. Creating value

    f. Delivering value

    g. Communicating value

    h. Conducting marketing responsibly for long-term success.

To take up the above tasks, the think-tanks of the marketing department need vast amounts of supporting information and reliable data about target market consumers/customers who are heavily involved in switching. Even though most of the personnel in marketing departments are actively engaged in the above tasks of marketing management, the main objective of any company or organization remains that of achieving profitability, at least in the medium and long run.

Process of Marketing Management

The marketing department is the most crucial, and the entire success or failure of the organization mostly depends on the marketing department because of its contribution to the profit figure and the lone highest revenue-generating department in most companies. The marketing management is the process of (a) *planning* marketing activities, (b) directing the *implementation* of the plans, and (c) *controlling* these plans. Successful marketing departments invest a vast amount of time and effort, which need to be managed effectively with significant efficacy. For professionally managed companies, marketing is an ongoing process that has no beginning and no end. Before initiating the planning process, the marketing department analyzes the existing situation of the company—including a necessary review of the company's relative market share; competitors and their strengths and weaknesses; and the company's own strengths, weaknesses, opportunities, and threats. At the planning stage, the marketing department must decide on the position to be reached. What are the mission and objectives to be set for the coming financial year, along with the strategy to be implemented to achieve those objectives? At the implementation stage, marketing departments must concentrate on how they are going to put in action the entire strategy designed along with varied resource requirements to achieve the stated objectives. Necessarily, these objectives must meet the SMART principle. That is, each objective must be **S**pecific, **M**easurable, **A**greed-upon and achievable, **R**ealistic, and **T**ime-bound. In the final stage of evaluation and control, the higher officials concerned must carefully verify whether the actual results meet the stated objectives set at the beginning of the planning horizon. If the desired results are not met, what are the key reasons and contextual constraints? What prudent corrective measures are needed? A wise marketing team not only assesses the negative but also has ideas for positive performance through turnaround strategies. The process has a feedback loop to enable the identification of precise points of deficiency, and the need for appropriate corrective action.

    We introduce Figure 5.1 to depict precisely such a comprehensive step-by-step process of marketing management and the relationship among the steps involved. In the following sections of this chapter, an exposition is provided around the five stages of the marketing management process.

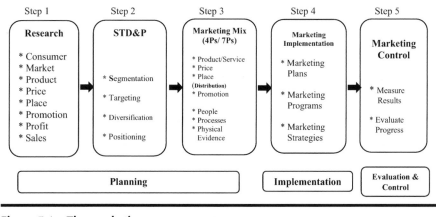

Figure 5.1   The marketing management process.

Marketing Research

To make the best possible preemptive decisions in the short run and strategic choices for the long run, marketers need timely, accurate, and actionable information on so many issues. Before going to market any product or service, marketing teams essentially need a lot more information about target market customers, their buying motives and spending patterns, market growth rate, as well as the company's market structure and competitors. Market structure considerations are important. The only companies that do not need to worry about competition are monopolies. There are precious few of these in the world. After that, whether the market structure is a duopoly (two companies, such as Etisalat and Du being the two telecommunication firms in the United Arab Emirates), or oligopoly, monopolistic competition or a purely competitive structure, one has to pay attention to the strategic moves of rival companies lest they take market share away from you.

Other considerations companies need to take into account as part of their industry audit or environmental, external scanning are the organized and unorganized sectors, as well as other macroenvironmental elements such as cultural, social, economic, legal, and governmental issues—generally done under what is called the PESTEL Analysis: **P**olitical, **E**conomic, **S**ocial, **T**echnological, **E**nvironmental, and **L**egal factors. For gathering all the required data, marketing think-tanks must depend on marketing research data along with other sources like internal records, marketing intelligence, analyzing the environment through which there is a possibility to garner information about the required products and services from the target markets under what is known as the *Marketing Concept*. Marketing research is all about generating insights that provide diagnostic information about how and why specific factors influence the markets and what that means to marketers. Marketing research is more comprehensive and is different from market research in which research teams should collect information about the specific demand and its dynamics. Marketing research is the systematic gathering, recording, analyzing the data related to any marketing issues, particularly product/service, price, place, promotion, consumer, market, sales, as well as profit profiles.

The American Marketing Association (AMA, 2017b) defines marketing research as

> the function that links the consumer, customer, and public to the marketer through information—information used to identify and define marketing opportunities and problems; generate, refine, and evaluate marketing actions; monitor marketing performance; and improve understanding of marketing as a process.
>
> Marketing research specifies the information required to address these issues, designs the method for collecting information, manages and implements the data collection process, analyzes the results, and communicates the findings and their implications.

This definition of marketing research was adopted by the AMA in 2017.

In Figure 5.1, step one highlights information about the scope of marketing research. If any marketing department needs any specific information about consumers, markets, products/services, prices, distribution, and much more, through marketing research they can collect the most relevant and pertinent information. While gathering research information on any said issues, a six-step process to conduct marketing research would be helpful to take advantage of all the resources and practices available. Good marketers adopt a formal marketing research process (Kotler and Keller, 2018). The specific steps are as follows: (a) define the problem, the decision alternatives, and the research objectives; (b) develop the research plan; (c) collect the information; (d) analyze the data; (e) present the findings; and (f) make the decision. The most crucial step is the second one involving the research plan. The entire success or failure of the process depends largely on how effectively and efficiently the researcher develops the research plan. In brief, the research plan should consist of information about (a) data sources, (b) research approaches, (c) research instruments, (d) sampling plan, and (e) contact methods.

A. *Data sources*: the researcher should first decide on different primary or secondary sources (or both) to gather the data relevant to the research.
B. *Research approaches*: Marketers can gather data in five different ways: (a) *Observational study*: where researchers can collect data by seeing customers at the time of shopping or consuming products; (b) *Focus group research*: Focus groups are a gathering of 6–12 people selected from the close culture or vicinity for known demographic, psychographic, or other considerations and organized to debate on various matters at length, for a small payment; (c) *Survey research* is another research approach in which the researcher collect the data by administering either questionnaires, in-person, by phone, or

via online means; (d) *Behavioral research*: is the study of the many personal issues or variables that influence the creation of one's habits, which have a significant impact because they affect so many areas of one's daily life; however, (e) *Experimental research* is strictly confined to the scientific research designed to capture cause-and-effect relationships by eliminating competing explanations of the findings (Kotler and Keller, 2018).

C. *Research instruments*: Most of the marketers' widely used research instruments are questionnaires, qualitative measures, and technological devices. (a) *The questionnaire* is the most popularly known research instrument, which consists of a series of questions to collect information from the subjects. (b) *Qualitative measures* mainly focus on the collection of verbal data rather than measurements to gain a deep understanding of a topic, and qualitative measures mostly deal with textual data or words. (c) *Technological devices* like galvanometers and tachistoscope flashes are more visual technologies widely administered by the researchers, mainly in the developed world.

D. *Sampling plan*: After careful selection of data sources, research approach, and instruments, the marketing researchers must concentrate on designing a sampling plan that addresses three crucial decisions, viz., (a) *sampling unit* (Whom should we survey?), (b) *sampling size* (How many people should we study?), and (c) *sampling procedure* (How should we choose the respondents?).

E. *Contact method*: Finally, the marketing researcher should decide on how to contact the subject or respondent to gather the required information—will it be via mail, by phone, in person, or will this be done online?

Segmentation, Targeting, Differentiation, and Positioning (STD&P)

After collection of required information through research, in the process of designing a customer-driven marketing strategy, the marketing department now concentrates on two most critical issues viz., (a) select customers to serve (segmentation and targeting) and (b) decide on the value proposition (differentiation and positioning). The designing of a segmentation, targeting, differentiation, and positioning (STD&P) strategy, which is a business strategy, plays a vital role in getting the right customers to the company's range of products and services. Based on the limitation, companies cannot connect with large, broad, or diverse markets due to its heterogeneity in nature, which is going to be an extra burden both financially and non-financially along with the risk of failure. Market segmentation makes it easier for companies to reach their target market consumers with specific needs and wants, which would benefit the company, in the long run, to administer all kinds of resources more effectively and more strategically.

Market segmentation is nothing but the dividing of the total heterogeneity nature of the market into various homogeneous sub-sets of the market base on *geographical* (nations, states, regions, counties, cities, or neighborhoods), *demographical* (age, family size, family life cycle, gender, income, occupation, education, religion, race, genera-tion, nationality, and social class), *psychographic* (buyers divided into groups based on psychological/personality traits, lifestyle, or values), and *behavioral tendencies* (atti-tude toward, use of, or response to a product) to understand consumers better.

Once the company has identified its market segmentation, the company must decide how many segments and which one to target to reach the company's objec-tive. "*Market targeting* consists of evaluating each market segment's attractiveness and selecting one or more market segments to enter." A target market is a set or group of customers sharing similar everyday needs, wants, and aspirations and characteristics that the firm chooses to focus on. Based on convenience, most of the marketers are progressively combining numerous variables to identify smaller, better-defined target groups. While selecting the attractive market segments, the firm should concentrate on two critical factors, namely, the segment's overall attrac-tiveness and the company's objectives and resources. The potential market segment should have attractiveness in its size, growth rate, profitability, scale economies, and low risk profiles that exist along with the company's objectives and resources.

In the final two steps, differentiation and positioning, companies will decide on a value proposal regarding how it will create value for target market consum-ers. Companies exist not for the short-run, but for long-term purposes. Whenever they have kept in mind the long-term orientation in their investment, no company can win if its products and services resemble every other product and offer on the market unless it can create a sense of "different-ness" and uniqueness about its prod-ucts in the minds of the consumer. As part of the strategic marketing management process, each offering must represent the right kinds of things in the minds of the target market. *Differentiation* involves showing the superior and notable distinc-tion of the company's products/service to create excellent customer value. Ries and Trout (2000) defined *positioning* as the act of designing a company's offering and image to occupy a distinctive place in the minds of the target market." The main objective of the positioning is to create a unique location or slot in the consumer mind with an everlasting impression to maximize the potential advantage to the company. While choosing the differentiation and positioning strategies, companies have first to identify a set of possible sustainable benefits to build a position, decide on the right competitive advantage, and finally, select the overall positioning strat-egy. Differentiation and positioning are the ways consumers define the product on important attributes such as product differentiation, service differentiation, chan-nels, people, brand image, quality, design, features, technology, ease of use, and ease of application when compared to competing products.

Marketing Mix (4Ps and 7Ps) Including the Updated

A marketing expert named E. Jerome McCarthy first coined the 4Ps of mar-keting in the 1960s and classified marketing activities into *marketing-mix* tools of four broad kinds, which he called the *four Ps* of marketing: product, price, place, and promotion (McCarthy and Perreault, 2002). The marketing mix defined by Kotler and Armstrong (2016) views the concept as a "set of tactical marketing tools that the firm blends to produce the response it wants in the target market." The competent designing and introduction of 4Ps/7Ps in target markets is an important framework for executing of strategic marketing plans with a clear eye on customer satisfaction and profitability. The marketing mix definition is straightforward, and it is laying the right product or a combination thereof in the right place, at the right time, and at the right price. The marketing mix is predominately associated with the 4Ps of marketing, the 7Ps of service marketing, and the 4C theories developed in the 1990s (https://marketingmix.co.uk/). By the 1980s, several marketing theorists and practitioners were calling for an expanded and modified marketing mix framework, particularly for services marketing. With an extensive discussion held in the American Marketing Association's 1980s conferences, Booms (1981) proposed a model of 7Ps, comprising the original 4Ps plus process, people, and physical evidence, as being more applicable for services marketing.

1. *Product*: A product is anything that can be offered for sale in the market to satisfy the needs, wants, and aspirations of a group of people. The product can be intangible or tangible or sometimes maybe in the form of services. While designing a challenging and competing product, the firm's marketing managers have to concentrate on product quality, design and style, features, branding, packaging, sizes, services, warranties, and returns.
2. *Price*: Price is the only marketing mix element that provides revenues to the organization in which marketing managers must show some extra cautious approach in designing products/services in terms of list price, discounts, allowances, payment period, and credit terms. In simple terms, price is the value of a product/service expressed in terms of money, which decides the company's revenue, profits, and its very survival.
3. *Place*: The third P of the marketing mix includes both channels of distribution and physical distribution. The channels of distribution are the route or way chosen by the marketer to move the finished product from the manufacturer to the final consumer and with the proper selection of channels, coverage, and assortments. Physical distribution includes all the activities associated with the supply of finished products to the final consumer and includes such crucial functions as order processing, inventory control, warehousing and storage, transportation and logistics, and customer service.
4. *Promotion*: The fourth P of the marketing mix, promotion, describes all those activities that are designed by the producer to influence buyer behavior through diverse communication, namely, advertising, sales promotion, personal selling, public relations, publicity, events and experiences, direct and database marketing, online and social media marketing, and mobile marketing.

The Services Marketing Mix: The services marketing mix (also known as an extended marketing mix) is a combination of the unique elements of services marketing that enterprises employ to communicate their managerial and service brand message to customers. The services marketing mix assumes the service as a product itself, and it adds three more Ps which are required for best service delivery. The extended services marketing mix includes People, Process, and Physical evidence and are within the control of the firm and essentially needed to influence the customer's initial decision to purchase a service, along with the customer satisfaction and repurchase decisions.

5. *People*: People means all human actors who are involved as a part of service delivery to influence buyer behavior, that is, service personnel, customers, and other customers in the service environment. People or employees in service organizations are the epicenter of the quality delivery of services and need to have the best talents to continue influential interactive marketing with the target market consumers. Service companies' success or failure depends to a large degree on how effectively people or employees deliver the expected level of service. Particularly, frontline employees who are responsible for handling customers are crucial in creating happy and returning customers.

6. *Process*: Process means the actual step-by-step procedure, mechanism, and flow of activities by which the service is delivered. The service delivery process enhances the customer experiences and the operational flow of the service. Service companies that introduce the quickest, most efficient, and the highest quality delivery process stand the best chance of winning the hearts of service markets and consumers.

7. *Physical evidence*: Physical evidence is the ambience in which the service is delivered where the service firm and consumer interact with one another. The physical evidence includes all of the tangible representations of the service such as brochures, letterhead, business cards, report formats, signage, employee dress code with identity cards, and equipment along with the physical facility where the service delivery has taken place just like the retail bank branch facility.

Updating Marketing Mix: Kotler and Keller (2018) updated the marketing mix elements with additional 4Ps of people, processes, programs, and performance. In the updated 4Ps, people and processes have already been explained above, while the two new ones of programs and performance are elucidated below.

8. *Programs*: Programs signify all the company's customer-focused actions. It comprises all the marketing mix activities, namely, product, price, place, and promotion, along with extended marketing mix elements like people, processes, and physical evidence. These 4Ps/7Ps are either online or offline, conventional or unconventional. These marketing mix elements should be integrated in such a way as to achieve **synergy** $(2+2=5)$ whereby their whole is greater than the sum of their parts to achieve multiple objectives of the firm at the same time, with the profit motive being the most important.

9. *Performance*: Performance examines how well a company's marketing activities compete in the marketplace. Kotler and Keller (2018) defined performance as holistic marketing, to capture the range of possible outcome measures that have financial and nonfinancial implications (profitability, as well as brand and customer equity) and impacts beyond the company itself (social responsibility, legal, ethical, and the environment). Finally, these new four Ps apply to all disciplines within the company, and by thinking this way, managers are supposed to more closely align themselves with the rest of the company.

Marketing Implementation

Managing any operative function of management, including marketing, requires planning, implementation, and control of the specific functional area. In the process, after preparation, execution is the most crucial and critical area of management. Its key elements are not limited to projects; procedures; resource allocation; and structural, behavioral, functional, and operational decisions. Related to the marketing function, whatever the plans, policies, programs, systems, strategies, and budgets prepared and introduced to achieve a specific objective(s) require deep concentration, commitment, and coordination from all the employees of the intra- and inter-departmental functional areas of the business. The success of any strategy, including marketing strategy, essentially needs an enthusiastic approach at the implementation stage from all levels of employees. According to Bonoma (1985), marketing implementation is the process that turns marketing plans into action assignments. It ensures that such tasks are executed in a manner that accomplishes the plan's stated objectives. Any marketing strategy implementation is first treated as a project in which the department develops proper plans, programs, and budgets for perfect execution. In the next stage, the implementation follows the procedural framework, which consists of several legislative enactments and administrative orders, besides the policy guidelines issued by the respective levels of governments in any country from time to time. In the next stage of marketing implementation, the top management of the department deals with the procurement and commitment of financial, physical, and human resources to the accurate application of all the strategic tasks for the achievement of marketing and organizational objectives. The marketing strategy implementation also requires the introduction of regulatory, structural modifications, and adjustments for the accurate and timely application along with committed leadership with unique behavioral tendencies like leadership qualities, corporate culture and policies, use of power, personal values, business ethics, and social responsibility. Finally, the accurate and thoughtful marketing strategies implementation needs the highest degree of intra- and interfunctional commitment along with concentration on operational execution through proper processes and people, with the expected level of pace to achieve the expected level of productivity.

Marketing Evaluation and Control

A systematic marketing evaluation offers a yardstick for monitoring marketing activity and highlights recommendations to improve the efficiency and performance of the company's marketing activity. It is crucial and provides business with an opportunity to reflect on the marketing department's performance relative to the goals of the department. The marketing evaluation refers to the comprehensive and systematic analysis, evaluation, and interpretation of the business environment, both internal and external, its goals, objectives, and strategies. Kotler and Keller (2018) defined marketing control as "the process by which firms assess the effects of their marketing activities and programs and make necessary changes and adjustments." The marketing control is of four types: (a) Annual-plan control examines whether the planned results are being achieved or not. The top and middle management are responsible for annual-plan control through sales analysis, market share analysis, sales-to-expense ratios, financial analysis, and market-based scorecard analysis; (b) profitability control investigates where the company is making and misplacing money through the verification of profitability by product, territory customer segment, trade channel, and order size and marketing controller is responsible for checking the profitability of the company; (c) efficiency control assesses the spending efficiency and influence of marketing costs by sales force, advertising, sales promotion, distribution, and line and staff management, and marketing controllers are responsible for checking the efficiency control of the marketing department; (d) strategic control scrutinizes whether the company is tracking its most exceptional prospects with respect to markets, products, and distribution channels through the approaches of marketing effectiveness rating instrument, marketing audit, marketing excellence review, and company ethical and social responsibility reviews.

Data Analytics in Marketing

A fully operational business will record a vast amount of data in its day-to-day service. This recorded data, which is often confidential, piles up within a short time. Several crucial and critical insights can be derived by analyzing the historical data of any business which triggers the upscale of the business and its service to the consumer. Predicting the company's performance based on its historical operations can be a substantial beneficial tactic for the present day's operations. Observing the result of this data analysis, marketing academics, managers, public policy-makers, or an executive of an organization ponder the fruitful decisions after observing the result of its data analysis. Data scientists habitually use the traditional pipeline while mining the data. Data mining is the process of automatically discovering useful information in large data repositories (Tan et al., 2019). To be precise, data analysis is the practice of measuring, managing, and scrutinizing marketing performance to amplify its effectiveness and optimize the return on investment.

Understanding marketing analytics allows markets to be more efficient at the jobs and diminish wastage. Marketing data mining is an integral part of Knowledge Discovery in Databases (KDD), which is the overall process of converting the raw data into useful information. In general, the data science pipeline includes data pre-processing, data modeling, and data visualization. The input data can be stored in a variety of formats and may reside in a centralized data repository or be distributed across multiple sites based on diverse factors such as the operating department in an organization. According to Tan et al. (2019), not all information discovery tasks are considered to be data mining. Examples include queries, e.g., looking up individual records in a database or finding web pages that contain a particular set of keywords. The acquired marketing data should be keenly examined, which slides into the data processing phase in the data science pipeline.

Data Preprocessing

The purpose of the data preprocessing phase is to transform the raw input data into an apt format for the ensuing analysis. Blending the data from all the available sources is followed by cleaning the data, which includes steps such as noise reduction, omitting duplicates, and selecting records and features that are relevant to each data mining task. This stage in the data mining pipeline is the most time- and effort-consuming step and perhaps the most laborious in the entire KDD process.

As a crucial part of the data science pipeline, the marketing data analyst has to have the maximum possible knowledge about the data, which is ready to be analyzed. The type of data and the quality of the data are vital ingredients to understand the nature of the analysis to be done, and the conclusions to be made along with managerial and policy implications to be drawn. Marketing data can contain both numerical and categorical variables. The categorical attributes, that is, qualitative attributes, are further classified as nominal and ordinal. On the other hand, numeric attributes are further classified as either interval or ratio. The quality of the data will be analyzed based on several issues, such as the existence of noise and outliers, and missing, inconsistent, or replicate data. The quality of the result of the data analysis is directly proportional to the quality of the data in this stage. Using appropriate data cleaning techniques will upscale the overall quality of the data and sequentially the quality of the result of the analysis. Data quality is affected throughout the process at the initial data creation stage, that is, during the data entry stage. The measurement error, which is defined as a common problem at the value recorded stage, differs from the real value to some extent. The noise inside the data is another critical issue affecting data quality. Noise in the data can be easily understood when considering marketing data in time series format and spatial context format. Outliers are the marketing data that affects the quality of analysis significantly. According to Tan et al. (2019), the outliers in the marketing data "can appear as data objects that, in some sense, have characteristics that are different from most of the other data substances in the data set or values of an attribute that are unusual concerning the typical values for that attribute." Unlike noise in the marketing data, outliers can be legitimate data objects or values. Missing values in the data is also a prevalent scenario in marketing data. Handling missing values is one of the principal vital tasks because these missing values can mislead the model to a large extent. On the other hand, all missing values in a dataset cannot be treated equally. Some missing values can be ignored, whereas some missing values were absent due to human error that cannot be ignored.

Data preprocessing steps should be applied to make the data more suitable for data mining and to escape from issues affecting the data quality. Data aggregation, data sampling, dimensionality data reduction, feature subset selection, feature creation, discretization and binarization, and variable transformation are the most powerful techniques used in data cleaning in order to maintain high-level data quality. Used appropriately, these procedures can help the marketing data to be clean sequentially, and it is very beneficial toward getting fruitful data to result from the data modeling stage. An excellent performing model result will ultimately prompt a profitable marketing decision in an organization. Ultimately, that is a real benefit to the entire organization.

Data Modeling

Data modeling is a stage of developing machine learning models. As the name suggests, the machine learning model is a process of making a model learn and adapt the historical marketing data so that it can be eligible for making either predictions or classification based on each task. The machine learning models are trained using one or a combination of numerous statistical algorithms. According to Kuhn and Johnson (2013), modern approaches to model building split the dataset into training, testing, and validating datasets, which has been shown to find more optimal tuning parameters often and give a more accurate representation of the model's predictive or classification performance. The "training dataset" is the general term for the samples used to create the model, while the "test" or the "validation" dataset is used to qualify its performance. However, there is no general rule of thumb to illustrate the partition; the data must be split. In this scenario, the model's performance is also based on the amount of data used to train and test the model; consequently, it results in the problem of model overfitting. In addition to learning the general patterns in the data, the model has also learned the characteristics of each sample's unique noise. This type of model is said to overfit. Ideally, the model should be evaluated on samples that were not used to build or fine-tune the model so that they provide an unbiased sense of model effectiveness.

The simplest way to split the data into a training and test set is to take a simple random sample. However, there are more powerful sampling techniques to be used on the machine learning model, which can significantly upscale the performance of the model. These resampling techniques, such as K-fold cross-validation, generalized cross-validation, repeated training, and testing data splits, and the bootstraps are some of the widely known methods for the modeling.

Model tuning is another choice to consider getting the best model's performance possible. There are some parameters in some of the machine learning models which allow the analyst to tweak the values of the parameters instead of default values. Tuning the parameters very often upscales the model's performance and helps the model to make better and more accurate classification and prediction decisions. For instance, in the case of K-nearest neighbor algorithms, the K value is used to identify the K closest data points in the training data. To test and improve the model's performance, there is often a need to modify the K's value at each iteration of the model as it is executed.

Once the situations for the tuning issues have been determined for each model, the model selection is mainly dependent on the characteristics of the data and the type of questions being answered. There is an ample number of models available depending on each task. From the data point of view, they are classified as supervised and unsupervised machine learning models. Moreover, on the resulting point of view, the models are classified into regression models and classification models. Based on the usage of the suitable machine learning model's result, which is obtained from analyzing the marketing data, the responsible associate will be able to take or choose a decision of the desired task.

Customer Analytics

The Father of the Nation of India, Mahatma Gandhi, in his speech in South Africa in 1890, said that

> a customer is the most important visitor on our premises. He is not dependent on us. We are dependent on him. He is not an interruption of our work. He is the purpose of it. He is not an outsider in our business. He is part of it. We are not doing him a favor by serving him. He is doing us a favor by allowing us to do so.

This adage by Gandhi should be the philosophy well-worth engrossing and knocking at the heart of all customer interactions with business organizations. The total customer experience and satisfaction should be the present day's epitome of any business success irrespective of the magnitude and type of business wherever they are operating in the world. Marketing provides services in order to satisfy customers in every business. All businesses should develop an accurate mechanism to understand the entire range and types of customers with the assistance of customer analytics. Customer analytics (also known as customer data analytics) is an organized analysis of a firm's customer data and customer behavior to identify, attract, and retain the most profitable customers. Customer analytics plays a significant role in the prediction of consumer behavior.

Customer analytics is a procedure by which data from customer/consumer behavior is applied to assist in making key business decisions utilizing market segmentation and predictive analytics. Business houses employ analyzed customer information for conducting aggressive marketing to outperform rival competitors in their target markets. Based on the buying habits and lifestyle preferences obtained via customer analytics, businesses can create a separate consumer profile to generate the most profitable customer groups. The customer information comprises many aspects such as credit/debit card purchases, frequent preferences, magazine subscriptions, loyalty program memberships, surveys, and other in-store registrations. When many of these potential customers are accumulated with the back-up of customer analytics in an area, it indicates a fruitful place for the business to locate. Broadly, there are five types of customers, namely, consumers, resellers (all the middlemen), organizational customers, institutional customers, and international markets in the world, and most companies are always trying to serve all these to acquire more and more profits. All five types of customers have different buying motives, spending patterns, and factors influencing their buying behavior based on which companies are going to design and develop their business and marketing strategies to win the hearts of the customers. Customer analytics comes in handy in providing concrete analyzed data about the said information regarding each type of customer the business is planning to serve.

In any organization, there are three types of decision-makers involved in customer analytics at three levels. These are (a) developing a company strategy, (b) a marketing strategy, and (c) an operational-level strategy. (1) *Strategic decision-makers*: are the higher officials or people in the think-tank of the organization, notably the Chief Executive Officer (CEO), the Chief Operating Officer (COO), Board of Directors, and other functional Vice-Presidents who design and create the overall company strategy after the careful analysis of all the necessary data related to customers, competitors, markets, as well as micro- and macroenvironmental elements. To accomplish the same, customer-centric information is needed to make the best possible plan for how to run the company in the future. (2) *Marketing and sales decision-makers*: These are the people who occupy the top positions in the department. Typically, they include the marketing vice-president, and other managerial positions in charge of sales, marketing research, pricing, distribution, promotion, and general administration of the marketing function. In line with the strategic decisions of the organization, marketing and sales strategy is designed by the functional decision-makers in any organization. The marketing and sales strategy deals with getting new customers along with the existing customers by delivering quality products and services, which provide maximum satisfaction with the most suitable price and availability. (3) *Operation decision-makers*: are individuals who implement the market and promotion activities normally in sales and distribution network areas. The decision support they entail is in terms of whom to sell to, what, when to sell, and what to say to retain dissatisfied customers. These frontline managerial cadres are the users of the operational information, which includes marketing and customer databases, marketing and sales performance reports, customer and sales tracking information to plan, report, and conduct various analyses.

Customer analytics is the means of analyzing customer data collected across departments in an organization for evaluating, recognizing, and deciphering customer behavior across several phases in their buying process. Done properly, customer analytics leads to better, informed, and data-driven decisions and attaches various data points and establishes trends, patterns, differences, and gaps. The basic concept in customer analytics is the application of technology on the data collected to get some actionable insight from it, which will help the company to make better decisions that can drive better marketing results and ROI. Furthermore, customer analytics facilitates improving customer reaction to the company's promotional activities, consolidates customer loyalty, and accordingly enhances sales returns and tightens the company's overall promotional expenditure by letting the organization emphasize on customers who are most likely to make a purchase/perform the desired action. It helps the firm to identify unsatisfied customers and prevent brand detraction. To get more customer insights, every company has to set up a vigorous customer analytics framework that necessitates a powerful technology stack to get more detailed information about the type of customers, buying motives, spending patterns, and much more. Every company must design three key processes for planning customer analytics. These are: (a) Know customers: Here, companies must define objectives and map customer journeys. (b) Collect relevant data from touchpoints such as company website, in-store visits, and purchases, email clicks, app activities, blog communities, social media, CRM systems, other internal and external systems. (c) Define outcomes in a descriptive, prescriptive, predictive manner by elaborately diagnosing the complete customer information.

According to Sauro (2015), the efforts and activities of product development, marketing sales, and services are directed to anticipate and fulfill customer needs. The term *customer analytics* illustrates a list of actions and tasks. This list includes gathering data, using statistical machine learning models to detect the patterns, finding the insight, supporting decisions, and optimizing the customer journey. The four highly contrasting tasks making customer analytics different from the regular statistical analysis is that customer analytics is more customer-focused at the individual customer level, and longitudinal, behavioral, and attitudinal in nature. Using an apt way of analyzing the customer-related data, the benefits for an organization include streamlined campaigns, competitive pricing, customization, reduced waste of capital, faster delivery of service to the customer, and consequently higher profitability by having more and better loyal customers. Customer analytics is vastly used in almost all industries, including retail, finance, online, and software. It is, above all else, a global phenomenon.

Chapter Conclusions and Implications

This chapter aims to enhance the level of awareness of the intellectual and technical issues surrounding the analysis of massive marketing data related to different issues. The first part of this chapter, "Data Analytics in Marketing and Customer Analytics" evidently highlights information about the definitions of core concepts like data and business analytics, marketing and marketing management, customer and consumer along with the significance of marketing and customer analytics. In the second part of this chapter, various responsibilities and processes of marketing management are explained and presented diagrammatically with elaborate definitions and information. The most crucial information about data analytics in marketing is expounded in detail in the third part of this chapter with relevant information about customer analytics. Massive data analysis is not the province of any one field. However, it is instead a meticulously interdisciplinary business. More effective solutions to massive marketing data analysis will require an intimate blending of ideas from computer science and statistics, with essential contributions also needed from applied and pure mathematics, from optimization theory, and information theory. The enormous marketing data analysis establishes novel challenges at the interface between humans and computers. The analyzed data input proffers reliable and valid information to the decision-makers of the organization in general and marketing departments in particular. Ultimately, the key concepts and processes described in this chapter—*which are applicable at both national and international levels*—call for careful management and marketing attention toward customer needs and customer satisfaction, in pursuit of greater revenue, greater profits, growth, and survival.

Acknowledgments

The first author Dr. Raj owes a great deal to the inspirational and transformational leader of the College of Business, Al Ghurair University Dean, Prof. Gerry N. Muuka, along with other faculty and admin colleagues and also indebted to my inspiration Dr. Sophia Johnson for motivating me to write this chapter. Dr. Raj is indebted uniquely to the Government of Dubai and Dubai Health Authority and also expressly grateful to Dr. Sasi Kumar and Dr. Said Shah, other Doctors, nursing and laboratory staff of Rashid Hospital and Al Rahaba Care Center for their incessant, indomitable, and indefatigable five-star medical services to COVID-19 patients in Dubai. Dr. Raj is admiring of his wife Aruna and son Mr. Lohith Sekhar (Data Scientist-UCSD, USA), who provided time, support, and other ways and means needed to prepare this chapter.

Finally, we would like to express our sincere gratitude to the professional efforts and chapter publishing opportunity given by the Chief Editor Dr. Mounir Kehal and Dr. Shahira El Alfy of the Higher Colleges of Technology in the UAE, as well as Taylor & Francis Group/CRC Press.

References

American Marketing Association. *AMA Dictionary: Customer*, April 2014. Accessed March 18, 2020. https://marketing-dictionary.org/c/customer/.

American Marketing Association. "Definition of marketing." 2017a. Accessed March 18, 2020. https://www.ama.org/the-definition-of-marketing-what-is-marketing/.

American Marketing Association. "Definition of marketing research." 2017b. Accessed March 19, 2020. https://www.ama.org/the-definition-of-marketing-what-is-marketing/.

Bonoma, T.V. *The Marketing Edge: Making Strategies Work*. New York: Free Press, 1985.

Booms, B. "Marketing strategies and organizational structures for service firms." *Marketing of Services*, (1981).

Common Language in Marketing Project, 2016. Accessed March 18, 2020. https://marketing-dictionary.org/m/marketing-analytics/.

Drucker, P. *Management: Tasks, Responsibilities, Practices*. New York: Harper and Row, 1973, pp. 64–65.

Farris, P. W., N. Bendle, P. E. Pfeifer, and D. Reibstein. *Marketing Metrics: The Definitive Guide to Measuring Marketing Performance*. Upper Saddle River, NJ: Pearson Education, 2010.

Kioumarsi, H., Z. S. Yahaya, A. W. Rahman, M. Abdelrahman, P. U., Aikhuomobhogbe, A. M. Orheruata, et al. "Customer satisfaction: The case of fresh meat-eating quality preferences and the USDA yield grade standard." *Asian Journal of Animal and Veterinary Advances* 6, no. 12 (2009): 52–59.

Kotler, P. and G. Armstrong. "Principles of marketing with my marketing lab: Global edition, 16/E." (2016).

Kotler, P. *Marketing Management, (Millennium Edition)*. Custom Edition for University of Phoenix. Upper Saddle River, NJ: Prentice Hall, 2000, p. 9.

Kotler, P. and K.L. Keller. *Marketing Management, Global Edition*. Harlow: Pearson Education UK, 2016.

Kotler, P. and K.L. Keller. *Marketing Management, Global Edition*. Harlow: Pearson Education UK, 2018.

Kuhn, M. and K. Johnson. *Applied Predictive Modeling*, Vol. 26. New York: Springer, 2016.

Laursen, G.H.N. and J. Thorlund. *Business Analytics for Managers: Taking Business Intelligence Beyond Reporting*. Hoboken, NJ: John Wiley & Sons, 2016.

Liberatore, M.J. and W. Luo. "The analytics movement: Implications for operations research." *Interfaces* 40, no. 4 (2010): 313–324.

Lichtenstein, S., D.H.B. Bednall, and S. Adam. "Marketing research and customer analytics: Interfunctional knowledge integration." *International Journal of Technology Marketing* 3, no. 1 (2008): 81–96.

The Marketing Mix. "The marketing mix 4P's and 7P's explained." Accessed April 11, 2020 https://marketingmix.co.uk/.

McCarthy, E. J. and W. D. Perreault. *Basic Marketing: A Global-Managerial Approach*, 14th edition. Homewood, IL: McGraw-Hill/Irwin, 2002.

Ries, A. and J. Trout. *Positioning: The Battle for Your Mind*, 20th Anniversary Edition. New York: McGraw-Hill, 2000.

Runkler, T.A. "Data analytics." *Wiesbaden: Springer* 10, (2012): 978-3. doi:10.1007/978-3-658-29779-4.

SAS. "Customer analytics: What it is and why it matters." 2020. Accessed March 19, 2020 https://www.sas.com/en_ae/insights/marketing/customer-analytics.html.

Sauro, J. *Customer Analytics for Dummies*. Hoboken, NJ: John Wiley & Sons, 2015.

Tan, P.-N., M. Steinbach, A. Karpatne, and V. Kumar. *Introduction to Data Mining*. New Delhi: Pearson Education, India, 2019.

Chapter 6

Marketing Analytics

Tabani Ndlovu and Sihle Ndlovu
Higher Colleges of Technology

Contents

Introduction

Marketing analytics involves the forensic use of data to generate a more detailed and insightful understanding of customers and their life journey, particularly at every point of interaction with providers of products and services (Arunachalam and Sharma, 2019; Hauser, 2007). Data is therefore central in marketing analytics as it offers the source of detailed customer insights to better understand and predict customer behaviours as well as help to infer future customer intentions and trends which enable organisations to respond with appropriate and competitive marketing offers. To generate meaningful insights, marketers have to 'mine, analyze, interpret, and present the information so that it is converted into actionable intelligence. In this process, the customer's information DNA is tracked, segmented, modelled and then acted upon' (Hauser, 2007, p. 1). Marketing analytics therefore presents a potentially potent arsenal that organisations could deploy for marketing prowess in this digital age where information is power and a source of competitive responsiveness for organisational success (Keszey and Biemans, 2017; Lane and Levy, 2019). Developments in technology have seen an explosion in the amount of data that is captured about customer purchase patterns, behaviours, reactions to marketing stimuli, loyalties, etc., owing to widespread use of social media channels, digital tools and various software applications that help keep track of customer trends and preferences (Wedel and Kannan, 2016).

New marketing techniques have emerged alongside the exploding volumes of customer data, including such techniques as 'recommendations, geo-fencing, search marketing, and retargeting' among others (Wedel and Kannan, 2016, p. 97). This presents the marketing field as a fertile area promising further growth and innovation, lending itself to new possibilities as the technological frontiers continue to broaden, heralding in new opportunities in the areas of machine learning, artificial intelligence and big data.

While the availability of phenomenal amounts of consumer data (big data) has been a welcome move, it has not come without its challenges (see, for example, Amado et al., 2018; Fan, Han and Liu, 2014; Leeflang et al., 2014). The plethora of data volumes gathered about customers can be overwhelming, causing possible confusion as to what is useful and what is not. Such data is akin to a mine where one has to sift through layers of rubble before they can strike seams of usable rich ore. This has given rise to such terms as data mining. Pursuant to the above, despite well-documented benefits of deploying marketing analytics to better appraise the effectiveness of various organisational marketing activities and how these help to better understand customer preferences, gauge competitive activity, predict marketing trends, as well as accurately capture market potential among others, take-up of marketing analytics still remains very low (Cao, Duan and El Banna, 2019; Arunachalam and Sharma, 2019). This raises questions as to whether organisations lack relevant expertise and resources or if they feel that this area does not lend itself usable in their contexts. This paper discusses the perceived paradox of the hyped-up benefits of marketing analytics vs. the real world low take-up and application of marketing analytics within the marketing field, raising questions about possible barriers or possible superficial understanding of the potential of marketing analytics. This paper then goes on to outline some of the benefits to be gained from more widespread use of marketing analytics before concluding by offering recommendations and a framework for implementation of and wider adoption of marketing analytics in marketing.

Insights from a Survey of Small and Medium Enterprises (SMEs) from the UK's East Midlands Region

This paper draws insight from a survey that was targeted at SMEs in the UK's East Midlands region, gauging their perceptions of and capacity to utilise marketing analytics techniques. Thirty SMEs responded to the survey that targeted those SMEs in the service sector. Although the sample was very small and not likely to accurately represent all SMEs, the results brought forth some insightful observations that will be highlighted in the study and do support the literature on marketing analytics and its deployment across the marketing field. Notable observations included the fact that only 13% of the respondents agreed that they had the requisite marketing expertise to deploy marketing metrics. Of the 13%, half of them used very rudimentary marketing metrics tools, demonstrating that even among those who claim to have expertise of deploying marketing metrics, there is a possibility that the understanding of the area is superficial. Of the total respondents, 30% indicated that they rely on third party data as they did not have capacity to generate, process and analyse data from their own sources to any meaningful extent other than providing traditional computations of sales, costs, profits, customer churn, etc. Their ability to predict with accuracy any future customer trends was thus limited.

This affected their effectiveness in proactively developing targeted marketing offers to anticipate customers' needs. Surprisingly, when questioned about the role of marketing analytics in organisational success, a whopping 90% indicated that marketing metrics had a huge potential in generating timely intelligence for informed marketing decisions. The views from the above study mirror those found in other studies which raise questions about why marketing analytics adoption is lagging behind its hyped-up perception in organisational success. This is further discussed in the section below.

The Paradox of the Perceived Impact of Marketing Analytics vs. Funding

While the prospective contribution of marketing analytics to business performance is overwhelmingly acknowledged (see, for example, Bauer et al., 2016; Xu, Frankwick and Ramirez, 2016; Fogarty, Jing and Harrison, 2019), its take-up has remained modest. The 2018 CMO report perhaps presented a paradoxical picture of the marketing analytics conundrum. The report projected a 198% increase in marketing budgetary allocations towards marketing analytics over three years from 2018 to 2021. Perceived contributions of marketing analytics to business success by marketing leaders for the same period (2018–2021) was a modest 4.1 score out of a possible total of 7. This dichotomy between the two above does not make sense but has been consistent since the CMO surveys explored the question dating back more than five years. Mela and Moorman (2018, p. 1) argued that marketers believed that the effect of analytics on marketing performance was about '4.1 on a seven-point scale, where 1 = not at all effective and 7 = highly effective. More importantly, this performance impact has shown little increase over the last five years, when it was rated 3.8 on the same scale'. This raises the question on whether marketing analytics remains an under-utilised area despite it being recognised as an area that could have significant impacts on marketing performance. If this is so, it remains to be determined why marketers feel they have to fund an area that they perceive to have only a modest contribution in reality.

This paper explores some of the possible reasons behind the continued investment into marketing analytics despite the perceived low yields from the area, teasing out possible barriers that may be dampening the impact of marketing analytics. Different scholars have highlighted a number of different possible barriers (Harrison et al., 2018; Moktadir et al., 2019). A selection of intertwined possible barriers to the adoption and effective implementation of marketing analytics as inferred from the survey findings of SMEs drawn from the UK's East Midlands region are summarised in Figure 6.1 below and discussed in the ensuing sections.

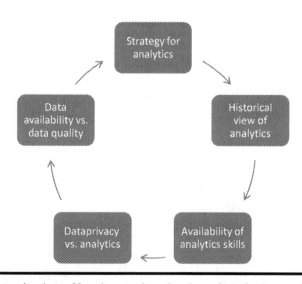

Figure 6.1   A selection of barriers to the adoption of marketing analytics.

Need for an Overarching Strategy for Marketing Analytics

Perhaps the starting point behind use of marketing analytics is an overarching strategy tying marketing analytics back to the business vision and mission. This is crucial as it offers the organisation a roadmap or template on what is required, how it should be undertaken, by who and for what purposes. A strategy prevents haphazard activities that lack coherence and fail to contribute towards the organisation's long-term vision. A strategy is crucial especially considering strict legal requirements around the handling of consumer data. It ensures that marketing analytics are not an add-on but a built-in element of overall strategic decision-making in the organisation (Huang and Rust, 2017; Marr, 2017). Sixty-three percent of the surveyed UK SMEs indicated that they had overarching strategies but considering their lack of marketing analytics expertise, it can be inferred that such strategies probably focused on use of traditional metrics and requisite analyses thereof for decision-making.

The Historical Use of Metrics and Analytics in Marketing

Metrics have traditionally not been enthusiastically adopted in the marketing domain with many organisations limiting performance measurement to sales volume, revenues, costs and profits (Kotler, Kartajaya and Setiawan, 2016; Mintu-Wimsatt and Lozada, 2018). Traditional metrics while providing useful historical information are backward-looking metrics and not very informative when planning ahead unless the future is assumed to be like the past (Lacasandile, Niguidula and Caballero, 2017). The lacklustre adoption of marketing analytics may be primarily attributed to a number of factors such as a limited appreciation of the potential existence of, and contribution of metrics and analytical tools (Fourati-Jamoussi and Niamba, 2016). Secondly, as discussed above, the subjects of marketing analytics and marketing metrics are relatively new in the curricula of many universities and business schools including business colleges. Consequently, many marketing graduates may not have had any educational background on both the theory and practice of marketing metrics and marketing analytics in relation to marketing performance as they may have followed more traditional routes that have not included marketing analytics (Osmani et al., 2019; Pitan, 2017).

Availability of Marketing Analytic Skills Specifically and Analytics Skills in General

In the 2018 CMO report, only 1.9% of surveyed marketing leaders indicated that they had adequate marketing analytic skills. The situation seemingly has remained the same since 2013 when the question on whether companies had the right marketing analysts was first asked. In a marketing analytics readiness study targeting SME in the UK's East Midlands region, out of the 30 SMEs who responded to the survey, only 4 (about 13%) indicated that they believed they had sufficient skills to employ use of marketing analytics. When questioned on which tools they used, all 4 out of 30 indicated that they mostly used free online marketing analytics tools and felt that employing more popular approaches such as Google Analytics was slightly beyond their scope and capacity at the time.

The numbers of marketing analytics-ready organisations is very low considering how big data is driving business transformation in today's digital age. Without competent and suitably-qualified analysts, marketing analytics will likely remain tokenistic or non-existent.

The above issue perhaps has its roots in business academic institutions churning out graduates whose areas of study do not embrace concepts such as marketing analytics (Wilson, McCabe and Smith, 2018). The section below explores the role of institutions of higher learning in designing and offering curricula that match the needs of the increasingly digitally-driven market.

Prevalence of Marketing Analytics Curricula in Business and Management Education

With fast-paced technological changes especially in the use of online marketing tools, it would appear academic institutions are on the backfoot in their attempts to design up-to-date curricula that address the needs of the dynamic marketing profession that now has to contend with big data and the advent of online marketing. According to Lasonde (2016), 71% of marketers have failed to find appropriately skilled marketers when recruiting. Added to that, a further 30% of marketing recruiters highlighted that finding and securing skilled marketing professionals was a big problem. Results drawn from the study referred to herein also revealed a very similar trend where 70% of the surveyed SMEs confirmed that they employed graduates with further and/or higher education qualifications with some marketing background. However, when questioned further about specific marketing analytics qualifications or skills, the study found that none of the graduates held such qualifications.

The above underscores the magnitude of the skills gap in the marketing field in general and specifically when one narrows this to online marketing and use of marketing analytics. Skilled professionals capable of mastering marketing analytics and its links to the emerging and evolving areas of artificial intelligence, cloud-based computing are increasingly in short supply (Ebert and Duarte, 2018; Hoberg et al., 2017; Kolding et al., 2018; Richardson and Bissell, 2019). The skills gap further deepens as one moves towards more niche and specialist areas of the digital marketing world as these are still relatively new and continuously evolving areas. There is therefore a direct correlation between courses taught at university and availability of skilled marketers. Lasonde (2016, p. 52) underscores this point 'The precipitous widespread interest in integrating data-driven marketing initiatives has outpaced talent creation, producing a marketing-skills gap'. The identified lag between curriculum development and responsiveness towards evolving digital market needs requires marketers to forge closer collaborations with institutions of higher learning so that such curricula can be developed and continuously updated to reflect the changing nature of business needs. Now more than ever, businesses need to take an active role in driving business education agenda. Such a partnership between business and education institutions ensures a tailored fit of educational courses and a steady flow of potential recruits who may also benefit from possible internships with businesses.

Higher education institutions (HEIs) such as the Higher Colleges of Technology (HCT) in the UAE are already engaging businesses to participate in the Industry Advisory Committees (IACs) where specific input is solicited from industry practitioners to directly influence the review and design of business courses. A similar approach is adopted by Nottingham Business School in the UK where Course Enhancement Boards comprise academics, business professionals, students, alumni and other stakeholders to review and enhance courses in line with latest stakeholder expectations and industry demands. Such approaches need to be embedded in the design of business curricula; otherwise, the skills gaps will continue to widen while HEIs continue to churn out graduates whose profiles may not match market needs (see, for example, Mintu-Wimsatt and Lozada, 2018). Another explanation of the low take-up of business analytics could be traced back to the historical use of analytics and metrics in marketing. This is discussed below.

Data Privacy vs. Analytics

The increased collection of consumer data has fuelled calls for more regulation on how such data is generated, stored and used (see, for example, Goddard, 2017; Mundie, 2014). There have been heightened concerns over consumer safety especially with the advent of online trawlers who can potentially phish on consumer data and prey on vulnerable, unsuspecting consumers. The GDPR (General Data Protection Regulations) have tightened requirements around how organisations process and store consumer data, especially ensuring that they get consent from such data subjects regarding how such data will be used (Goddard, 2017). This tightening of legislation throws spanners in the works of such data-reliant organisations as Facebook, Amazon, Google, eBay, among others, and requires them to have very strict procedures on ensuring the safety of consumer data. From an analytics perspective, availability of massive clouds of data makes analytics very easy and the more the data, the higher the accuracy of trends drawn from such data. If there are restrictions on the collection, use and storage of such data, this may slightly hamper marketing analytics, especially for smaller organisations. Undoubtedly, big organisations have the financial and legal muscles to navigate through the webs of legal statutes but smaller companies may find it difficult to weave their way around the increased legal obstacles (Houser and Voss, 2018).

Ninety percent of the surveyed SMEs from the UK's East Midlands region cited increased expenditure in responding to tightening legislative requirements as an additional business cost that they had to contend with. Given limited budgetary constraints for most SMEs, they may well opt not to venture into data-intensive pursuits in fear of possible cost escalations, and this may have negative effects on their marketing analytic activities (Zervakos, 2016).

Data Availability vs. Data Quality

While the issue of the availability of skills has been highlighted earlier as a big contributor to the low uptake of marketing analytics, availability of data is also a major concern for decision-making, especially in small and medium-sized organisations (Puklavec, Oliveira and Popovič, 2018; Singh and Radhakrishnan, 2019). The surveyed SMEs overwhelmingly identified data concerns as ranking among the top ten business challenges facing SMEs in the UK. This challenge may not be unique to UK SMEs as their characteristics are largely similar although the legislative requirements around data may be different across different countries. Accessing high-quality data cost-effectively is a challenge for a small business that may not have finely tuned strategies of how to go about this. For most small businesses, especially family-run and operated businesses that utilise whatever resources they can get from family members, there may be no or at best a weak strategy seeking to utilise data and inform marketing decision-making. Sixty percent of the surveyed UK SMEs pointed out that they were largely reliant on skills from family members but that there were graduates contributing more up-to-date trends and informing decision-making. For organisations that may not have access to such new and upcoming skillsets and unable to access paid services, they may struggle to access quality affordable data to make informed marketing decisions. Where the data is available, there is still need for expertise to mine through the data and determine what data are useful and what are not. Added to this burden, the tightening regulatory requirements around privacy may scare small businesses. Notwithstanding the above challenges, SMEs do not have a choice but to face these challenges head-on if they are to survive in this increasingly data-driven business world. The sooner they conduct honest and critical self-appraisals, the better they are able to start building the skills they require so as to better meet the ever-changing needs of this digital market.

Critical questions to be addressed centre around the following: What is the concerned company's data strategy and what data are needed for marketing decision-making? How can such data be obtained (*inhouse vs. outsourcing* – cost benefit analysis)? What data is already available and what are the different sources? What is the cost of such data and how does this compare with the perceived benefits of the data? Once data are accessed, what should be done with the data and how, to what effect? What tools are needed to manipulate the data to generate meaningful insights? Are the tools in question available and how much will it cost to access them?

Accessibility of Paid Professional Analytics

Despite the seemingly limited availability of competent marketing analysts, there are various professional organisations offering marketing analytics consultancy services. These are, however, few and far between and in most cases, their services are perceived to be beyond the reach of many small- and medium-sized organisations that desperately need this service. Further, marketing analytics consultancy services could be promoted more widely so that smaller organisations get to know about them and their services. From the surveyed SMEs in the UK's East Midlands region, only 40% of them indicated that they were aware of consultancy organisations offering specialised services in the areas of marketing analytics. Of those who responded, 68% indicated that often consultancy services were out of reach for them, and hence they opted to do basic data crunching in-house even though they acknowledged that they lacked intricate knowledge of marketing analytics. Given the above backdrop, there are questions to be asked about the future of marketing analytics considering the lacklustre operationalisation yet backdropped by increasing funding of the area. The section below explores the future of marketing analytics.

The Future of Marketing Analytics

While the take-up of marketing analytics is still low relative to projections, the future appears seemingly bright, especially considering the increased funding of this area which should help develop capacity and attract talent. This is further encouraged by the competitive nature of the job market with increasingly attractive perquisites offered to skilled professionals especially those straddling the digital and business professions (see, for example, Grundke, Marcolin and Squicciarini, 2018; Taylor-Smith et al., 2019; Ahmed et al., 2017). Compounding the above, developments in technology, social media platforms, software applications, machine learning and artificial intelligence and their increased applications in marketing settings, this promises to be a new frontier for marketing innovation and building of more intimate and sustained relationships with customers. These new frontiers promise new and more efficient deployment of technological tools to better understand customer trends, generate meaningful insights about customer responses to various marketing offers such as adverts, promotions, etc., so as to determine what efforts yield better results – all in an instant. Generation of insights around customer churn offer opportunities for repositioning offers responsively to better serve customers with appropriately tailored solutions and start new relationships with customers (Booth, 2019). Notwithstanding the positive outlook ahead, organisations need a structured approach of employing use of marketing analytics, ensuring that they lay all the necessary foundations for successful generation of marketing insights. This is discussed in the section below, employing use of a marketing analytics pyramid, denoting the hierarchical nature of the different elements required to fully implement marketing analytics.

The Typology of Marketing Analytics – Laying the Foundation

To benefit from the large volumes of data, organisations have to be endowed with expertise to sift through this data and sort it, to select what is usable and thereafter, make sense of it – which is where marketing analytics comes in as a way of generating marketing intelligence, a key ingredient for informed marketing decision-making. Viewed from this perspective and taking the feedback and suggestions of surveyed UK SMEs on what they perceived to be the foundations of successful deployment of marketing analytics, the usefulness of marketing analytics comes several steps down the line and requires some pertinent foundations to be lain before it can be effectively deployed. Figure 6.2 presents a pyramid of marketing analytics, situating the area on requisite antecedents which act as the anchoring bedrock on which a successful marketing analytics approach can be built.

Figure 6.2 The typology of marketing analytics antecedents (Adapted from The Data Co (2020, np)).

Overarching Strategy/Vision/Leadership

Any successful marketing strategies should be inspired from the very top of the organisation and aligned to the organisation's vision and mission (Sathi, 2017). This ensures that such strategies are entwined with the DNA of the organisation and appropriately sponsored at the highest levels of the organisation if they are to get traction from the generality of the organisation's troops and get requisite funding. Suggestions from the survey highlighted that it is very beneficial if marketing is represented at the highest levels in the organisational hierarchy so that marketing pursuits are accurately and faithfully articulated.

Resources/Competency/Capacity/Tools

Pursuit of, and deployment of, marketing analytics requires suitable investment. Organisations therefore need to effectively appraise themselves to determine if they have the necessary financial resources to be able to hire requisite talent and acquire the different tools, software applications and licences necessary to deploy marketing analytics. This is a challenge especially for small businesses that may not have sufficient financial resources nor the required skills and competencies to implement this. This area is not a 'one size fits all', and therefore, each organisation should be able to find cost-effective approaches that are suited to its situation and context. Most importantly, the issue of resources, competencies and skills must be linked back to the leadership's vision for the organisation and the envisaged strategy for metrics.

Data Availability vs. Data Quality

As has been pointed out earlier, organisations today are inundated with voluminous amounts of data making it difficult to determine which of this data are useful and which are not. At the same time, not all of the vastly available data are of the quality required to make informed decisions. This requires care and skill to sift through and select the data that can help generate meaningful insights. There is often a paradox where some marketing analysts receive huge amounts of data but complain about the dearth of quality marketing data. This requires organisations to fine-tune their data collection strategies by aligning them to the aspirations of the organisation so that time and resources are not wasted collecting data that will later be discarded as it is of no use.

Context

Organisations today operate in very dynamic environments where the shelf-life of data can be very limited. This suggests that there is a need for timely collection, processing and use of marketing information to address current and emerging contextual issues.

Data is only useful if it can help address issues surrounding an organisation. This means that the data should be current. Marketing analytics therefore should be contextually fashioned to deliver meaningful and timely insights in the specific context of each organisation. Analysts are therefore advised to avoid following approaches adopted by other organisations as their circumstances shape the choices and approaches they take.

Meaning and Marketing Intelligence

Marketing analytics are deployed for the benefit they give the organisation in generating meaningful insights that enable the organisation to make informed decisions about which customer groups to target; with which products and services, what customers' future preferences may be; patterns/trends; how to position such as well as differentiating the organisation and its offers from those of competitors. To generate such insightful meanings, the organisation needs all the previously discussed rungs of the marketing analytics pyramid covering a well-developed vision/mission, well-crafted strategy, adequate resources, competent personnel, appropriate marketing tools, clearly defined context with appropriately tailored techniques, all hinged on quality of available data and how this is synthesised to generate meaningful marketing intelligence that the organisation can act on with confidence.

Comments from the study participants highlighted the fact that a significant number of organisations attempt the deployment of marketing analytics without laying the requisite foundations discussed above. The result is a half-hearted attempt which may not yield any consistent quality information or at best, give patchy and uncoordinated pieces of information.

Conclusion

This paper has explored the dynamic marketing environment that uses latest software applications, digital tools and techniques and social media platforms to collect vast amounts of data about customer practices, behaviours, trends, among other things. Such data lends itself usable for analysis to generate marketing intelligence which can help guide marketing decision-making with high probabilities of accuracy. Unfortunately, as the data collected grows in volume and complexity of scope, it becomes difficult to analyse manually and requires use of advanced digital approaches and techniques. This is where marketing analytics come in. A study of SMEs based in the UK's East Midlands region together with various extant sources however indicate that despite the hyped-up potential role of marketing analytics in ramping up business performance, its impact is yet to be realised. This is against a backdrop of increased expenditure on marketing analytics. This paper used insights from the survey to elicit views on some of the barriers to the adoption of marketing analytics and uncovered a number of possible reasons including lack of overarching strategies, expertise, resources and quality data, among other factors.

This study further elicited views on what study participants believed to be the solutions towards the dearth of marketing analytics in business and results were utilised to construct a pyramid hierarchically positioning different antecedent elements that should underpin a marketing analytics strategy. Questions surrounding the low take-up of marketing analytics are far from over especially considering the limited availability of courses that focus on the area. This is further compounded by suggestions that the rate at which courses are developed may be slower than the rate at which the digital landscape is changing, suggesting that skills gained from institutions of higher learning may be obsolete by the time students graduate such that they need new skills when they join the world of work – if they work in the digital landscape in general and marketing analytics specifically. This is an area for further research as this study did not specifically focus on that.

References

Ahmed, S., Taskin, N., Pauleen, D.J. and Parker, J., (2017). Motivating information technology professionals: The case of New Zealand. *Australasian Journal of Information Systems*, *21*(1), pp. 1–30.

Amado, A., Cortez, P., Rita, P. and Moro, S., (2018). Research trends on big data in marketing: A text mining and topic modelling-based literature analysis. *European Research on Management and Business Economics*, *24*(1), pp. 1–7.

Arunachalam, S. and Sharma, A., (2019). Marketing analytics. In *Essentials of Business Analytics* (pp. 623–658). Springer Nature, Cham.

Bauer, T., Fiedler, L., Jacobs, J. and Spillecke, D., (2016). The secret to great marketing analytics? Connecting with the decision makers. *Forbes*, *6*, pp. 28–33.

Booth, D., (2019). Marketing analytics in the age of machine learning. *Applied Marketing Analytics*, *4*(3), pp. 214–221.

Cao, G., Duan, Y. and El Banna, A., (2019). A dynamic capability view of marketing analytics: Evidence from UK firms. *Industrial Marketing Management*, *76*, pp. 72–83.

Ebert, C. and Duarte, C.H.C., (2018). Digital transformation. *IEEE Software*, (4), pp. 16–21.

Fan, J., Han, F. and Liu, H., (2014). Challenges of big data analysis. *National Science Review*, *1*(2), pp. 293–314.

Fogarty, D., Jing, L. and Harrison, P., (2019). Using marketing analytics for improved health engagement and outcomes. *Applied Marketing Analytics*, *4*(4), pp. 300–310.

Fourati-Jamoussi, F. and Niamba, C.N., (2016). An evaluation of business intelligence tools: a cluster analysis of users' perceptions. *Journal of Intelligence Studies in Business*, *6*(1), pp. 37–47.

Goddard, M., (2017). The EU General Data Protection Regulation (GDPR): European regulation that has a global impact. *International Journal of Market Research*, *59*(6), pp. 703–705.

Grundke, R., Marcolin, L. and Squicciarini, M., (2018). Which skills for the digital era? Returns to skills analysis. *OECD Science, Technology and Industry Working Papers*, *2018*(9), pp. 1–37.

Harrison, D.E., Ajjan, H., Hair Jr, J.F., Risher, J., Petrescu, M. and Krishen, A.S., (2018). Advanced analytics: The impact on marketing and evolution from descriptive to predictive. In *Back to the Future: Revisiting the Foundations of Marketing*, Jie G. Fowler and Jeri Weiser, eds. Society of Marketing Advances, West Palm Beach, FL, pp. 206–207.

Hauser, W.J., (2007). Marketing analytics: The evolution of marketing research in the twenty-first century. *Direct Marketing: An International Journal, 1*(1), pp. 38–54.

HCT, (2020). Industry Advisory Committees. Available at: http://news.hct.ac.ae/en/2014/03/admc-host-hct-industry-advisory-council-meeting/, Last accessed: 15/06/2020.

Hoberg, P., Krcmar, H., Oswald, G. and Welz, B., (2017). Skills for digital transformation. Available at: http://idt. in.tum.de/wp-content/uploads/2018/01/IDT_Skill_Report_2017. Pdf, Last accessed: 15/06/2020.

Houser, K.A. and Voss, W.G., (2018). GDPR: The end of Google and Facebook or a new paradigm in data privacy. *Richmond Journal of Law and Technology, 25*, p. 1.

Huang, M.H. and Rust, R.T., (2017). Technology-driven service strategy. *Journal of the Academy of Marketing Science, 45*(6), pp. 906–924.

Keszey, T. and Biemans, W., (2017). Trust in marketing's use of information from sales: The moderating role of power. *Journal of Business & Industrial Marketing.*

Kolding, M., Sundblad, M., Alexa, J., Stone, M., Aravopoulou, E. and Evans, G., (2018). Information management–a skills gap? *The Bottom Line.*

Kotler, P., Kartajaya, H. and Setiawan, I., (2016). *Marketing 4.0: Moving from Traditional to Digital.* John Wiley & Sons, Hoboken, NJ.

Lacasandile, A.D., Niguidula, J.D. and Caballero, J.M., (2017), Mining the past to determine the future market: Sales forecasting using TSDM framework. In *TENCON 2017-2017 IEEE Region 10 Conference* (pp. 461–466). IEEE.

Lane, K. and Levy, S.J., (2019). Marketing in the digital age: A moveable feast of information. *Marketing in a Digital World (Review of Marketing Research), 16*, pp. 13–33.

Lasonde, J., (2016). Trends survey data shows major talent shortages across industries. Bullhorn. Retrieved from http://www.bullhorn.com/blog/2016/03/recruiting-talent-in-talent-shortages/.

Leeflang, P.S., Verhoef, P.C., Dahlström, P. and Freundt, T., (2014). Challenges and solutions for marketing in a digital era. *European Management Journal, 32*(1), pp. 1–12.

Marr, B., (2017). *Data Strategy: How to Profit from a World of Big Data, Analytics and the Internet of Things.* Kogan Page Publishers.

Mela, C.F. and Moorman, C., (2018). *Why Marketing Analytics Hasn't Lived Up to Its Promise.*

Mintu-Wimsatt, A. and Lozada, H.R., (2018). Business analytics in the marketing curriculum: A call for integration. *Marketing Education Review, 28*(1), pp. 1–5.

Moktadir, M.A., Ali, S.M., Paul, S.K. and Shukla, N., (2019). Barriers to big data analytics in manufacturing supply chains: A case study from Bangladesh. *Computers & Industrial Engineering, 128*, pp. 1063–1075.

Mundie, C., (2014). Privacy pragmatism; focus on data use, not data collection. *Foreign Affairs, 93*, p. 28.

NBS, (2020). Course Enhancement Boards. Available at: https://www.ntualumni.org.uk/getting_involved/alumni_fellowship_programme/application_form, Last accessed: 15/06/2020.

Osmani, M., Weerakkody, V., Hindi, N. and Eldabi, T., (2019). Graduates employability skills: A review of literature against market demand. *Journal of Education for Business, 94*(7), pp. 423–432.

Pitan, O.S., (2017). Graduate employees' generic skills and training needs. *Higher Education, Skills and Work-Based Learning.*

Puklavec, B., Oliveira, T. and Popovič, A., (2018). Understanding the determinants of business intelligence system adoption stages. *Industrial Management & Data Systems.*

Richardson, L. and Bissell, D., (2019). Geographies of digital skill. *Geoforum, 99*, pp. 278–286.

Sathi, A., (2017). *Engaging Customers Using Big Data: How Marketing Analytics Are Transforming Business.* Springer.

Singh, H. and Radhakrishnan, V.T. (2019). *Method and system for facilitating real-time data availability in enterprises.* U.S. Patent Application 15/837,765.

Taylor-Smith, E., Smith, S., Fabian, K., Berg, T., Meharg, D. and Varey, A., (2019), Bridging the digital skills gap: Are computing degree apprenticeships the answer? In *Proceedings of the 2019 ACM Conference on Innovation and Technology in Computer Science Education* (pp. 126–132).

The Data Co, (2020). Three important elements of marketing analytics. Available at: http://www.thedata.co/3-important-elements-marketing-analytics-success/, Last accessed: 14/06/2020.

Wedel, M. and Kannan, P.K., (2016). Marketing analytics for data-rich environments. *Journal of Marketing, 80*(6), pp. 97–121.

Wilson, E.J., McCabe, C. and Smith, R.S., (2018). Curriculum innovation for marketing analytics. *Marketing Education Review, 28*(1), pp. 52–66.

Xu, Z., Frankwick, G.L. and Ramirez, E., (2016). Effects of big data analytics and traditional marketing analytics on new product success: A knowledge fusion perspective. *Journal of Business Research, 69*(5), pp. 1562–1566.

Zervakos, N.E., (2016). *The cost of regulations for small businesses in California* (Doctoral dissertation, Capella University).

Chapter 7

Big Data Analytics

Sujni Paul

Higher Colleges of Technology

Contents

Some slogans of famous big data scientist is given below to throw more light on big data.

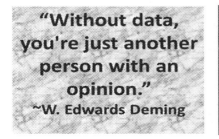

"Without data, you're just another person with an opinion."
~W. Edwards Deming

"Without big data analytics, companies are blind and deaf, wandering out onto the web like deer on a freeway."

- Geoffrey Moore

"Big Data: The next frontier for innovation, competition, and productivity"
(McKinsey Global Institute)

Characteristics of Big Data

Every year 2.5 quintillion bytes of data is produced. Big data are extremely large data sets that are so complex and unorganized. These large data sets are analyzed computationally to reveal patterns, trends related to human behavior and interactions. The three types of data are structured, semi-structured, and unstructured.

Structured data are organized and labeled into a formatted repository typically a database, so that its elements can be addressed for analysis that is more effective. Example is an Excel database.

Unstructured data are unknown forms, which are difficult to organize and very hard to classify. Typical examples of unstructured data are heterogeneous data source words in a text, emails, pictures, videos, and also the output produced by a Google search. Algorithms are used to identify this called Natural Language Processing. Semi-structured is a combination of the two. Sometimes it is seen as a structured form but it is actually not defined, for example, table definition in RDBMS, XML data. Also in Twitter the number of followers and the number of tweets are structured, whereas the content or images shared are unstructured (Figure 7.1).

Started up with the 5 Vs and now it is suggested to be a 7 V big data as described below (Figure 7.2).

Big data in Fighting COVID-19

Every big data has played a vital role in fighting COVID-19. Many countries used big data that helped them to reduce cross-infections, allowing the countries to get back to work and stabilize their economy. Big data was used to collect information

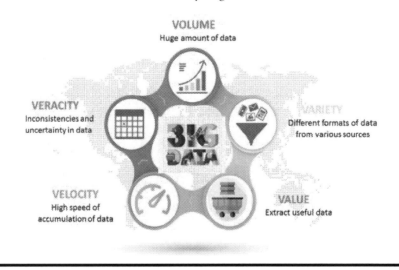

Figure 7.1   The 5 Vs of big data [1].

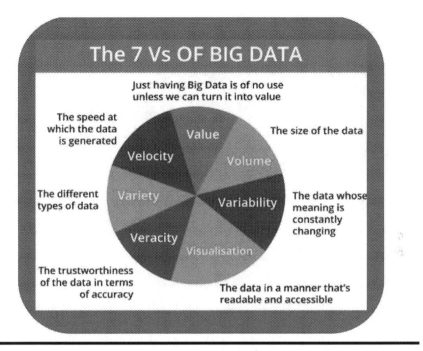

Figure 7.2   The 7 Vs of big data [2].

for different other types of health crises also earlier [3]. Algorithms were used to estimate the probability that any given individual has chances of getting COVID-19 by matching a user's mobile location to known infected hotspots. Different apps were used to see on a map the reported latest cases and give them the ability to avoid potential infection. In spite of different privacy issues, people tend to embrace big data because of its high-tech approach in dealing and fighting with COVID-19. It makes them understand the affected areas and necessity steps to be taken to slow down the spread of the infection (Figure 7.3).

```
#Global spread on the world map using Folium # creating world
map using Map class
world_map = folium.Map(location=[11,0],
tiles="cartodbpositron", zoom_start=2,
max_zoom = 6, min_zoom = 2)
# iterate over all the rows of confirmed_df to get the lat/long
for i in range(0,len(confirmed_df)): folium.Circle(
location=[confirmed_df.iloc[i]['lat'], confirmed_df.iloc[i]
['long']], fill=True,
radius=(int((np.log(confirmed_df.iloc[i,-1]+
1.00001)))+0.2)*50000, color='red',
fill_color='indigo',).
add_to(world_map) world_map
```

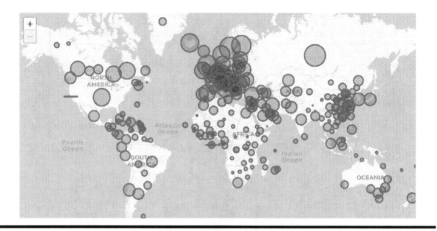

Figure 7.3   Simple data analysis done in Python with the big data [4].

Big Data in Artificial Intelligence

Ten years down the line, we were deep in the big data revolution when the volume, velocity, and variety of data completely overwhelmed the systems used to store, manipulate, and analyze that data. Now we're in the midst of an artificial intelligence (AI) revolution, but it's important to remember that big data hasn't gone away. Instead, big data has become the new normal. It's everywhere and in fact, it's only the big data that makes AI possible. When people think about advanced data work these days, the mind is immediately drawn toward AI and machine learning the way that the mind was automatically drawn towards big data a few years ago. Hence AI is a field in computer science, and it's the field that focuses on techniques that allow computers to do things typically done by humans like play a game of Go or classify photos or analyze MRIs, and all these are usually done in a way that shows adaptability to new circumstances.

Machine learning, on the other side, is a collection, a rubric of algorithms that can find patterns in data to predict outcomes. For example, whose face is this and is this the person that owns the phone? Machine learning improves over time as and when new data comes in and especially when there is more labeled data where you know what the particular outcome is. Also machine learning algorithms go from the relatively simple technique like a linear regression to the amazingly complex technique like a deep learning neural network. The connection between these fields can be understood clearly by looking at Google Trends search data over time, so this is showing us the relative popularity of searched terms over the last eight years from 2011 to 2019. The most important part is the one where the data scientist's needs generate a demand for change in data architecture, because this is the part where big data projects fail. When algorithms are computationally expensive or when infrastructure is not ready for ML algorithms. For instance, lately big banks in Brazil are hiring mainframe specialists to deal with this issue [5].

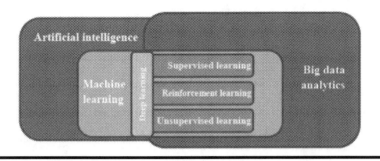

Figure 7.4 Schematic view of AI, big data, machine learning [6].

But here's what you need to know about the relationship between AI, machine learning, and big data. It shows that if AI and machine learning have thrived over the last few years, and they have, it is because they have stood on the shoulders of big data. So the relationship between these fields is in addition to that machine learning and AI are in addition to big data, not instead of it. They rely on big data; they can't do their work without it (Figure 7.4).

To elaborate it little further, AI requires massive data; the theory of neural networks has existed in the last few years that there has finally been enough data to make this work well. And that has to do with the volume, the first V of big data. Second, the data is streaming constantly especially with social media data and sensor media data, it's coming in tremendously, that's the velocity of big data that makes so much of the machine learning possible. And then finally, AI and machine learning involve many other types of novel data like images, movies, audio, and so many other things that don't fit into standard relational databases; that's the variety of big data where AI has been so useful [7]. And so, AI and machine learning have thrived because of the contributions of big data; the volume, velocity, and variety have made extraordinary developments within these respective fields.

Activities

The intelligent Piece of Paper

I am a highly intelligent piece of paper. Let's play tic-tac-toe.

Turing Test

This activity aims to get students thinking critically about what makes humans intelligent, and how computer scientists are designing computers to act more like us.

Big Data in Social Media and Internet of Things

The data revolution is growing very fast leading to a barely controlled explosion. The first major cause for this explosive growth is social media, and the second one is the Internet of Things. Though there are many others, these really play a starring role in the extraordinary growth of the big data world. To understand this more we have the uroboros, the snake that's feeding on itself which is just the same as social media because social media causes or begets more social media. Let's imagine a simple context, first a person puts post online, that post gets liked. Each like is an additional piece of data with a fair amount of metadata that goes with it. Another person puts an image online. That image gets tagged and it gets shared with anybody who's in it, and it gets put into forms that use the same tags, or somebody has a follower, they put something online and those followers share that content and multiply it, the reach of the post. The fact that more and more people are online and more and more people have social media profiles, and so there's this incredible growth. It's not just that it's doubling, it's multiplying across all dimensions. It just goes absolutely through the roof with social media.

Now, another one is the Internet of Things, that's IoT, and the classical examples of IoT include things like smart homes. Let's take an instance that I've got a smart thermostat that knows when we're home, it talks to our phones. It can tell what's going on. And maybe you've got lights and a security system and maybe you got a smart lock, and maybe you've got all sorts of other systems that are connected with each other. They're communicating constantly. And outside of the home, you can have a smart grid, where the city knows about the traffic levels; it knows about how much electricity is going between the generators and the various buildings and houses. It knows what's going on with the water system. There is so much information being exchanged here through sensors and networks which again leads to an explosive growth.

Another one that falls into this category is self-driving cars, which gather an extraordinary amount of data from the sensors they have all around them and they communicate to each other, and the time will soon come when they communicate directly with the road and with the traffic signals. There are so many different ways to gather all this data, and it gets even more complicated because the quality of the data has changed over time. You know, text comes first. When you send text messages, you started with your little flip phone and you sent your little, tiny text message, which actually was text. Text can be measured in kilobytes. But soon, for instance, you learn how to do audio and you can send a voice message or a sensor for your home can give you the audio about any information. That's usually measured in megabytes. And then, eventually, you get to video. Say, for instance, you have a doorbell. It's now giving you HD video over your phone of who's there at the door. Video can be measured in gigabytes. And so, we're not only increasing the number of things that provide the data, but we're climbing high up the ladder to kinds, or qualities, of data that are much, much larger and also might move from the structured to the large and unstructured format, again, from text to audio to video, and what those correspond to are the three Vs of big data: volume, velocity, and variety. And so, the social media revolution, which is still going on very actively, and the IoT, which again is still just at the beginning, have contributed massively to the explosive growth of data that constitutes both the challenge and really makes the fertile ground for the promise of big data.

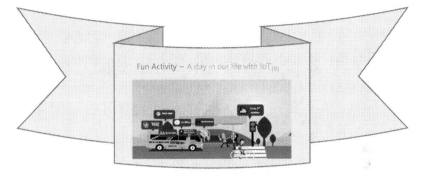

Big Data in Customer Interactions

In customer interaction, we see about what other people who are similar to them in some ways have done previously. You can do something like what have they searched for online, even when they weren't exactly in your own e-commerce sight. When you put together these profiles and you're trying to identify what a person is likely to buy, you need to be concerned about the accuracy of your predictions. If they're likely to respond to an advertisement and buy something, and if they actually are in your target audience, make sure to show it to them. So when you have a real candidate, make sure it triggers the response and you show them the thing that they want to see and that they want to get. With big data using Datameer reduces the customer acquisition cost. For example, a company correlated data on customer purchase histories, customer profiles, and customer behavior collected from social media sites indicating their personal interests. This data was then correlated with transaction histories and data on things that customers "liked" on Facebook to identify hidden patterns. These patterns enabled management to see that a large percentage of their high-value customers regularly watch the Food Network and shop at Whole Foods [9].

To balance things, you can only show advertisements to people who are likely to respond and buy something. You're wasting time and you're wasting money if you are showing advertisements and doing these engagements with people who have no interest in what you're doing. I mean, truthfully, anybody who done this and had an ad follow them around on the Internet, that's a false positive where they think you're a target and you're not. That makes customers feel like they're being stalked by some organization, and truthfully it's a creepy feeling. So you don't want to do that. You need to be more precise in your targeting and your categorization of potential customers.

So this is one of the main things that big data lets you do. The reason you can do that is because big data gives you more data sources. It's not just the database of who purchased what but they visited the site here. Here you get the unstructured data. Maybe you get some sort of information about the other sites they visit, maybe about information that they make public through comments on websites or posts that they share with other people. You get a wide range of more data sources that you can't analyze with normal methods. And by all these means when you have more data, you can identify things with greater precision, more accuracy. You can look at the edge cases and still have enough information to make a good decision. Also, you can be more sensitive to changes in a person's interest, the things that they've already bought, and the things that they've said online, the things that are happening all around them, and you can adapt to those changes in a more agile manner.

Here you can use your big data algorithms and results in particular situations. Now there are a few major benefits of using big data in these ways. First, your customers are more likely to feel heard, because they know that you have seen what they've said about you. They know you're paying attention to what they want. So feeling heard is mainly to be noted here. Then feeling understood. Not only are you monitoring what's going on, it makes sense to you and you're able to respond appropriately. Finally, you are also able to help your customers feel respected by offering them what they want in a manner that they want and not deluging them with other things that are irrelevant to them. So by using big data carefully in your customer interactions, your customers can feel heard, they can feel understood, and they can feel respected. And all together, those make you a company that they trust and a company that they are more likely to do business with in the future, which, after all, is your goal.

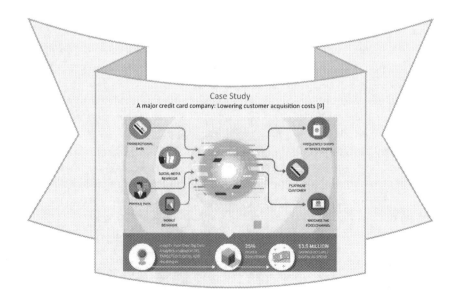

Big Data in Data Science

First, you must know the problem needed to solve. You may have a lot of data that you may think you will get some valuable insight from it. Hence for sure, patterns will emerge from those data.

The amount of digital data that exists is growing at a rapid rate, doubling every two years, and changing the way we live. An article by *Forbes* states that data is growing faster than ever before. By the year 2020, about 1.7 megabytes of new information will be created every second for every human being on the planet, which makes it extremely important to know the basics of the field at least [10].

Data science deals with structured and unstructured data that has everything that is related to data cleaning, preparation, and analysis (Figure 7.5).

There are a lot of data science tools to help in analysis. Windows Azure is a Spark and Hadoop service in the cloud. It offers good enterprise-grade security. Also Azure can be integrated with other productivity applications. It is very easy to deploy Hadoop in the cloud without purchasing new hardware or paying any other type of cost.

Figure 7.5   Data science vs. big data [10].

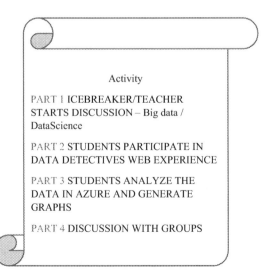

Activity

PART 1 ICEBREAKER/TEACHER STARTS DISCUSSION – Big data / DataScience

PART 2 STUDENTS PARTICIPATE IN DATA DETECTIVES WEB EXPERIENCE

PART 3 STUDENTS ANALYZE THE DATA IN AZURE AND GENERATE GRAPHS

PART 4 DISCUSSION WITH GROUPS

References

1. Ravi Kiran, "Big Data Characteristics: Know the 5 Vs of Big Data," August 20, 2019. Available at https://www.edureka.co/blog/big-data-characteristics/ [Accessed 10-10-2020].
2. Prathap Kudupu, Web Snippets, "7 Vs of Big Data," December 2018. Available at http://www.prathapkudupublog.com/2018/01/7-vs-of-big-data.html [Accessed 20-10-2020].
3. Bernard Marr Influencer, "The Vital Role of Big Data in the Fight against COVID-19" (Coronavirus) Published on April 19, 2020. Available at https://www.linkedin.com/pulse/vital-role-big-data-fight-against-covid-19-coronavirus-bernard-marr/ [Accessed 10-10-2020].
4. Fred N. Kiwanuka, "Data Analysis in Python using Big data", July 2020.
5. Matthew Mayo, "KDnuggets Machine Learning with Big Data Is, in Many Ways, Different than "Regular" Machine Learning," April 2020. Available at https://www.kdnuggets.com/2017/07/machine-learning-big-data-explained.html [Accessed 10-10-2020].
6. Okiriza Wibisono, Hidayah Dhini Ari, Anggraini Widjanarti, Alvin Andhika Zulen and Bruno Tissot1, "The Use of Big Data Analytics and Artificial Intelligence in Central Banking," 2019. Available at https://www.bis.org/ifc/publ/ifcb50.pdf [Accessed 20-10-2020].
7. Randy Bean, "How Big Data Is Empowering AI and Machine Learning at Scale?" May 08, 2017. Available at https://www.coursehero.com/file/36467729/How-Big-Data-Is-Empowering-AI-and-Machine-Learning-at-Scalepdf/ [Accessed 10-08-2020].
8. Fun Activity on IoT. Available at https://kit.ae/blog/article/smart-classrooms-thrive-with-iot [Accessed 20-10-2020].
9. 5 Big Data Use Cases to Understand Your Customer Journey, Datameer, Customer Analytics E-book. Available at https://docplayer.net/11715431-5-big-data-use-cases-to-understand-your-customer-journey-customer-analytics-ebook.html [Accessed 10-10-2020].
10. Avantika Monnappa, "Data Science vs. Big Data vs. Data Analytics," June 12, 2020. Available at https://www.simplilearn.com/data-science-vs-big-data-vs-data-analytics-article [Accessed 20-10-2020].

Chapter 8

New Product Development and Entrepreneurship Analytics

Kennedy Prince Modugu

Higher Colleges of Technology

Contents

Introduction

More than ever before, today's business environment is rapidly changing than it was some decades ago. This is largely due to increasing technological advancement and globalization. Therefore to survive and stay competitive, industry players must give priority to new product development (NPD) and innovation. This is because NPD is a critical success factor for most companies. According to Chen, Kang, Lee, Xing and Tong (2007), more than 50% of the sales in successful companies come from new products and more than 60% of the total revenue of most companies is attributable to new products. These assertions are testament to the multiplicity of new products that are available in everyday market. For example, each year, large multinational corporations such as Apple, Huawei and Microsoft launch new products into the market while gradually phasing out the old ones to pave way for increased market share. Same goes for companies producing consumables such as dairy products, juice, medicines and office stationery. It is also important to state that not all new products are a money-spinner for companies as the probability of product failure outweighs its success if the right measures are not taken.

Many new products witness high failure rates. About 40% of new products are estimated to fail at launch, even after all the development and testing work; out of every 7–10 new-product concepts, only one is a commercial success; and only 13% of firms report that their total new product efforts achieve their annual profit objectives (Cooper, 2019). Wide variances exist around these and other performance statistics, however, with the best performers doing dramatically better than the rest. A lot depends on the strategic handling of NPD process.

The Concepts of New Product and New Product Development

Attempt at defining what is and what is not a new product is not an easy task for both academics and industry practitioners. Many students of business management have had much fun arguing over whether the Sony Walkman was, indeed, a new product or merely repackage of an existing technology. Another example that illustrates this point is long-life milk, known in the United States as aseptic milk. This product has been consumed for many years in Europe, but it is a relatively new product for most consumers in the United States. Consumers who drink refrigerated milk may be extremely wary of milk sold from a nonrefrigerated shelf. Once again, whilst clearly this product is not absolutely new, it can be seen that it is more useful, from a product manager's perspective, to adopt a relativistic view.

It is important to note that a new product is a multidimensional concept. It can be defined differently and can take many forms. Some dimensions will be tangible product features and others intangible. One may ask whether the provision of different packaging for a product constitutes a new product. Surely, the answer may be yes or no. New packaging, coupled with additional marketing effort, especially in terms of marketing communications, can help to reposition a product. GlaxoSmithKline successfully achieved this with its beverage product Lucozade. Today, this product is known as a sports drink, yet older readers will recall that the product was packaged originally in a distinctive bottle wrapped in yellow cellophane and commonly purchased at pharmacists for sick children. This illustrates the difficulty of attempting to offer a single definition for a new product. Therefore, if we accept that a product has many dimensions, then it must follow that it is theoretically possible to label a product 'new' merely by altering one of these dimensions, for example, packaging (Trott, 2017). In addition, Corrocher and Zirulia (2010) observe that mobile communication operators use pricing tariffs to develop innovative new services. These alterations create a new dimension and, in theory, a new product, even if the change is very minimal. Indeed, Johne and Snelson (1988) suggest that the options for both new and existing product lines centre on altering the variables such as marketing, economics, production management, R&D, and design and engineering as depicted below.

i. Changing the performance capabilities of the product (for example, a new, improved washing detergent)
ii. Changing the application advice for the product (for example, the use of the Persil ball in washing machines)
iii. Changing the after-sales service for the product (for example, frequency of service for a motor car)

    iv. Changing the promoted image of the product (for example, the use of 'green'-image refill packs)

    v. Changing the availability of the product (for example, the use of chocolate-vending machines)

    vi. Changing the price of the product (for example, the newspaper industry has experienced severe price wars).

From the foregoing, a new product can be described as any product that has witnessed a variability in features, packaging, brand name, level of service, quality specifications, price and technology. Therefore, NPD consists of the activities of the firm that lead to a stream of new or changed product or market offerings over time. This includes the generation of opportunities, their selection and transformation into artefacts (manufactured products) and activities (services) offered to customers, and the institutionalization of improvements in the NPD activities themselves (Loch & Kavadias).

Classification of New Products

There have been many attempts to classify new products into certain categories. Very often, the distinction between one category and another is one of degree and attempting to classify products is subject to judgement. It is worthy of note, however, that only 10% of all new products are truly innovative. These products involve the greatest risk because they are new to both the company and the marketplace. Most new product activity is devoted to improving existing products. At Sony, 80% of new product activity is undertaken to modify and improve the company's existing products. The following classification identifies the commonly accepted categories of NPDs as argued by Trott (2017).

New-to-the-World Products

These represent a small proportion of all new products introduced. They are the first of their kind and create a new market. They are inventions that usually contain a significant development in technology, such as a new discovery, or manipulate existing technology in a very different way, leading to revolutionary new designs, such as Dyson's vacuum cleaner. Other examples include Apple's iPad, 3M's Post-it Notes and Guinness' 'in-can' system.

New Product Lines

Although not new to the marketplace, these products are new to the particular company. They provide an opportunity for the company to enter an established market for the first time. For example, Google, Sony and Microsoft have all entered the smartphone market to compete with market leaders Apple and Samsung.

Additions to Existing Lines

This category is a subset of new product lines above. The distinction is that, whilst the company already has a line of products in this market, the product is significantly different from the present product offering, but not so different that it is a new line. The distinction between this category and the former is one of degree. For example, Hewlett-Packard's colour ink-jet printer was an addition to its established line of ink-jet printers.

Improvements and Revisions to Existing Products

These new products are replacements of existing products in a firm's product line. For example, Hewlett-Packard's ink-jet printer has received numerous modifications over time and, with each revision, performance and reliability have been improved. Also, manufacturing cost reductions can be introduced, providing increased added value. This classification represents a significant proportion of all new product introductions.

Cost Reductions

This category of products may not be viewed as new from a marketing perspective, largely because they offer no new benefits to the consumer other than possibly reduced costs. From the firm's perspective, however, they may be very significant. The ability to offer similar performance whilst reducing production costs provides enormous added-value potential. Indeed, frequently it is this category of new product that can produce the greatest financial rewards for the firm. Improved manufacturing processes and the use of different materials are key contributing factors. The effect may be to reduce the number of moving parts or use more cost-effective materials. The difference between this category and the improvement category is, simply, that a cost reduction may not result in a product improvement.

Repositioning

These new products are, essentially, the discovery of new applications for existing products. This has as much to do with consumer perception and branding as technical development. This is, nonetheless, an important category. Following the medical science discovery that aspirin thins blood, for example, the product has been repositioned from an analgesic to an over-the-counter remedy for blood clots and one that may help to prevent strokes and heart attacks.

In practice, most of the projects in a firm's portfolio are improvements to products already on the market, additions to existing lines and products new to the firm, but already manufactured by competitors. Figure 8.1 illustrates the average project portfolio within firms. Here, 70% of new products are improvements, cost reductions and additions to existing lines.

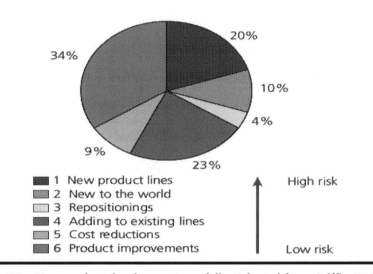

**Figure 8.1   New product development portfolio (Adapted from Griffin (1997), ©
John Wiley & Sons Ltd.)**

New Product Development Process

In order to stay successful in the face of maturing products, companies have to obtain
new ones by a carefully executed new product development process. Nevertheless,
they are confronted with some challenges as discussed in the introductory part of
this chapter. Out of the numerous products entering the development process only a
handful reach the market. Therefore, it is crucial to understand consumers, markets
and competitors in order to develop products that deliver superior value to customers.
In other words, there is no way around a systematic, customer-driven new product
development process for finding and growing new products. Figure 8.2 represents
the eight major steps in the NPD process.

Idea Generation Stage

The NPD process starts with idea generation. Idea generation refers to the systematic search for new-product ideas. Typically, a company generates hundreds of ideas,
maybe even thousands, to find a handful of good ones in the end. Two sources of
new ideas can be identified. The first is the internal idea sources where the company
finds new ideas internally through R&D and contributions from employees. The
second is external idea sources where the company finds new ideas externally. This
consists of all kinds of external sources, for example customers, distributors and
suppliers, as well as competitors. The most important external sources are customers, because the NPD process should focus on creating customer value.

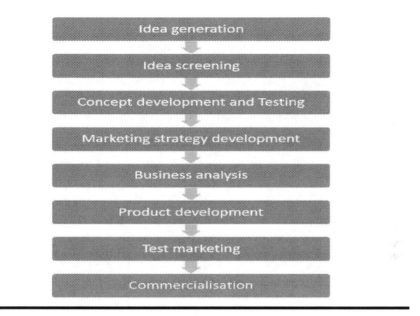

Figure 8.2   New product development process flowchart.

Idea Screening Stage

The next step in the NPD process is idea screening. Idea screening means nothing else than filtering the ideas to pick out the good ones. In other words, all ideas generated are screened to identify the feasible ones and drop those that the firm considers not feasible. While the purpose of idea generation is to create a large number of ideas, the purpose of the succeeding stages is to reduce that number. The reason is that product development costs rise greatly in later stages. Therefore, the company would like to go ahead only with those product ideas that will turn into profitable products. Dropping the poor ideas as soon as possible is, consequently, a crucial and timely action.

Concept Development and Testing Stage

To go on in the NPD process, attractive ideas must be developed into a product concept. A product concept is a detailed version of the new product idea stated in meaningful consumer terms. You should distinguish the following:

- A product idea – an idea for a possible product
- A product concept – a detailed version of the idea stated in meaningful consumer terms
- A product image – the way consumers perceive an actual or potential product.

Two parts of this stage are discussed in detail. They are *concept development* and *concept testing.*

Concept Development

Imagine a car manufacturer that has developed an all-electric car. The idea has passed the idea screening and must now be developed into a concept. The marketer's task is to develop this new product into alternative product concepts. Then, the company can find out how attractive each concept is to customers and choose the best one. Possible product concepts for this electric car could be:

- *Concept 1*: an affordably priced midsize car designed as a second family car to be used around town for visiting friends and doing shopping.
- *Concept 2*: a mid-priced sporty compact car appealing to young singles and couples.
- *Concept 3*: a high-end midsize utility vehicle appealing to those who like the spacious SUVs but also want an economical car.

As one can see, these concepts need to be quite precise in order to be meaningful. In the next sub-stage, each concept is tested.

Concept Testing

New product concepts, such as those given above, need to be tested with groups of target consumers. The concepts can be presented to consumers either symbolically or physically. The question is always: Does the particular concept have strong consumer appeal? For some concept tests, a word or picture description might be sufficient. However, to increase the reliability of the test, a more concrete and physical presentation of the product concept may be needed. After exposing the concept to the group of target consumers, they will be asked to answer questions in order to find out the consumer appeal and customer value of each concept.

Marketing Strategy Development Stage

The next step in the NPD process is the marketing strategy development. When a promising concept has been developed and tested, it is time to design an initial marketing strategy for the new product based on the product concept for introducing this new product to the market. The marketing strategy statement consists of three parts and should be formulated carefully:

- A description of the target market, the planned value proposition, and the sales, market share and profit goals for the first few years
- An outline of the product's planned price, distribution and marketing budget for the first year
- The planned long-term sales, profit goals and the marketing mix strategy.

Business Analysis Stage

Once decided upon a product concept and marketing strategy, management can evaluate the business attractiveness of the proposed new product. The fifth step in the NPD process involves a review of the sales, costs and profit projections for the new product to find out whether these factors satisfy the company's objectives. If they do, the product can be moved on to the product development stage.

In order to estimate sales, the company could look at the sales history of similar products and conduct market surveys. Then, it should be able to estimate minimum and maximum sales to assess the range of risk. When the sales forecast is prepared, the firm can estimate the expected costs and profits for a product, including marketing, R&D and operations. All the sales and costs figures together can eventually be used to analyse the new product's financial attractiveness.

Product Development Stage

The NPD process goes on with the actual product development. Up to this point, for many new product concepts, there may exist only a word description, a drawing or perhaps a rough prototype. However, if the product concept passes the business test, it must be developed into a physical product to ensure that the product idea can be turned into a workable market offering. The problem is, though, that at this stage, R&D and engineering costs cause a huge jump in investment. The R&D department will develop and test one or more physical versions of the product concept. Developing a successful prototype, however, can take days, weeks, months or even years, depending on the product and prototype methods.

In addition, products often undergo tests to make sure they perform safely and effectively. This can be done by the firm itself or outsourced. In many cases, marketers involve actual customers in product testing. Consumers can evaluate prototypes and work with pre-release products. Their experiences may be very useful in the product development stage.

Test Marketing Stage

The last stage before commercialization in the NPD process is test marketing. In this stage of the NPD process, the product and its proposed marketing programme are tested in realistic market settings. Therefore, test marketing gives the marketer experience with marketing the product before going to the great expense of full introduction. In fact, it allows the company to test the product and its entire marketing programme, including targeting and positioning strategy, advertising, distributions and packaging before the full investment is made.

The amount of test marketing necessary varies with each new product. Especially when introducing a new product requiring a large investment, when the risks are high or when the firm is not sure of the product or its marketing programme, a lot of test marketing may be carried out.

Commercialization Stage

Test marketing has given management the information needed to make the final decision: launch or do not launch the new product. The final stage in the NPD process is commercialization. Commercialization is the introduction of a new product into the market. At this point, the highest costs are incurred: the company may need to build or rent a manufacturing facility. Large amounts may be spent on advertising, sales promotion and other marketing efforts in the first year.

Some factors should be considered before the product is commercialized:

- *Introduction timing*: For instance, if the economy is down, it might be wise to wait until the following year to launch the product. However, if competitors are ready to introduce their own products, the company should push to introduce the new product sooner.
- *Introduction place*: Where should the new product be launched? Should it be launched in a single location, a region, the national market or the international market? Normally, companies do not have the confidence, capital and capacity to launch new products into full national or international distribution from the start. Instead, they usually develop a planned market rollout over time.

In all of these steps of the NPD process, the most important focus is on creating superior customer value. Only then, the product can become a success in the market. Only very few products actually get the chance to become a success. The risks and costs are simply too high to allow every product to pass every stage of the NPD process.

Product Development Analytics

Analytics is crucial to product management for one significant purpose: product improvement. Without analytics, product development would be reduced to a series of shots in the dark and product teams would be clueless as to how well their products were meeting user expectations.

The measurements taken by metrics and the insights provided by analytics enable product teams to make informed decisions about upgrading product functionality or adding capabilities. Without measuring and analysing the results, they would have no idea if the revisions implemented are effective or even necessary. They would be flying blind.

The five key roles of analytics in product development and management are:

Product viability: A variety of analytics tools can verify product concepts, helping developers test, learn, adjust and retest to speed up the product design and launch process.

Informed product decision-making: Analytics has made decision-making more objective, reliable and faster. While intuition based on experience and expertise can still play a valuable role in product development, it can and should take a backseat to objective analytics.

Product progress measurement: Product analytics can inform team members about which features are working and which are not. Analytics plays a critical role in creating an accurate product roadmap that can inform a firm of where their product is currently, where it wants it to be and how to get it there.

User experience insights: Product teams can use analytics to understand why users are buying their product and how they are using it.

Product development inspiration: Analytics can jump-start innovation and help an existing product remain viable for an extended period of time. Quantitative analytics, used in conjunction with qualitative techniques, can provide a more holistic view of a product to help product management teams make the kind of focused improvements and adjustments that will help maintain that product's value and improve its longevity.

Over the past decade or so, data generated by metrics and the analytical tools used to tease insights out of it have transformed product development and management. While some product team members may lament the demise of 'seat-of-the-pants' engineering, the reality today is that without data and the analytics to understand it, effective product development and successful product management are simply not possible.

Predictive Analytics in Product Development

Business analytics revolves around three domains, namely descriptive analytics, prescriptive analytics and predictive analytics. Descriptive analytics is the use of data to understand past and current business performance and make informed decisions. Prescriptive analytics, on the other hand, focuses on identifying the best alternatives to minimize or maximize some objectives. Predictive analytics predicts the future by examining historical data, detecting patterns or relationships in these data and then extrapolating these relationships forward in time.

Organizations have long relied on traditional product development tools and approaches, including FMEA, CAD simulations, design of experiments and value stream analysis, to heighten efficiencies, eliminate waste and optimize costs. However, given the ever-increasing volumes of data that flow into and through companies, conventional product development technologies and tactics are no longer sufficient. Although product developers continually look for better ways to handle the abundance of data at their disposal, most don't have the right tools to manage it, make sense of it or apply the insight it provides to support future product initiatives. Innovative companies know that data-driven insights and decisions can help improve all aspects of product development. According to McKinsey's global survey, many are already applying big data/analytics to:

Predictive Analytics Across the Value Chain

Ideation & Concept	Engineering & Design	Development & Validation	Pre-Production/ Commercialization	Launch & After-Market
Crowdsourcing and social media play a significant role in **collaborative product development**. Insights from suppliers' manufacturing processes and materials can aid in better design and **accelerate time to market**. Insights from previous product performance help in **maintaining the right product portfolio**. Analysis of intellectual property provides crucial information to **design a legally sound product**.	Product data provides information about how a particular component was designed, plus insights into challenges that were encountered. Logics and rules from this data will help **design new parts and assemblies** and promote standardization by harvesting old parts from existing databases. Insights from manufacturing equipment and processes help improve **"Design for Manufacturing."** BOM (bill of materials) analysis helps set the **right product cost**.	Insights concerning hazardous materials, legally restricted substances and small components, for example, help assure **regulatory compliance** and aid in **faster product development**. Data on transport conditions (weather, humidity, etc.) helps in **developing the right packaging contents**. Insights from quality inspections and third-party lab testing can provide vital information for **product design**.	Information on local laws helps assure appropriate **product/ packaging/labeling specifications**. Insights from local markets help in **launching customized variants** and fine-tuning products to **suit various consumer segments**. Cost insights from product development aid in **launching the product at the right price**. Customer data analytics help refine existing designs and develop **specifications for new models and variants**.	Best-in-class manufacturers can capture the data generated from warranty claims, spares, and service, and use it to **develop better products**. Product recalls, although very expensive, provide crucial insights into flaws in the product development process and **provide opportunity for correction**.

Figure 8.3 Analytics resources for start-ups (https://segment.com/catalog/ #integrations/analytics.)

- Improve research and development (R&D)
- Develop new product strategies
- Identify new market segments
- Deepen customer knowledge/relationships
- Improve customer segmentation and targeting.

Predictive analytics applies across the product development value chain as canvased by Joshi and Kansupada (2020) and depicted in the Figure 8.3 below.

Entrepreneurship Analytics

Since 1930s, entrepreneurship has been identified as a positive driving force for regional economic growth and development (Schumpeter, 1934). The progress of many countries is largely attributable to entrepreneurial activities and entrepreneurship-driven policies. To combat the growing unemployment rate in most emerging economies, attention has drastically shifted to youth entrepreneurship as a means of gainful employment for the teeming youth population of those countries. While entrepreneurship may be a sure bet for employment and growth, it is no doubt a herculean task to start and successfully manage a business through its thick and thin. Thanks to the advent of analytics that has transformed virtually all spheres of human endeavours, including entrepreneurship.

In business, analytics can be described as the use of data, information technology, statistical analysis, quantitative methods and mathematical or computer-based models. Data analytics techniques enable firms to use effectively such abundant data, giving SMEs a competitive edge and increasing their productivity such as reducing costs, enhancing marketing practices and strengthening their ability to identify or foresee trends (Bianchini & Michalkova, 2019).

However, SMEs and entrepreneurs face difficult challenges in accessing and analysing relevant data. On the one hand, limited digital skills by management and employees may fuel misperceptions on the actual risks and benefits deriving from adoption of recent digital technologies. On the other hand, small businesses typically find it more difficult to identify, attract and retain the specialists needed to deploy effective data analytics. In addition, SMEs also face limited financing options and burdensome regulatory requirements (for example personal data protection) often represent additional barriers for SMEs. Governments of nation are increasingly acknowledging the importance of data analytics for SMEs and are taking action to address these key challenges. Measures include offering training and skills development programmes to entrepreneurs and SMEs' employees; introducing regulatory reforms that contribute to enhanced data management practices by SMEs; promoting data sharing and diffusion; supporting knowledge exchange among SMEs, as well as public institutions, business associations and other stakeholders; and providing financial support for data analytics projects in SMEs.

Analytics for Start-up Entrepreneurs

One major source of trepidation for start-up entrepreneurs is how to navigate the vast data analytics ecosystem to identify what is suitable and convenient for their chosen business. The increasing number of new data analytics tools and proliferation of new terminologies further compound this fear. Data analytics is not as complex as some data scientists portray it. Most start-ups are well inadvertently involved in data analytics without necessarily deploying the latest technologies and tools. However, there are a vast array of analytics resources available to start-ups to leverage on as shown below (Figure 8.4).

The stage, nature and complexity of a business determine largely the sophistication of analytics tools required. It is, however, worthy of note that getting valuable and actionable data requires some more effort as this can be quite challenging especially for new entrants into the industry. Here are a few guidelines for start-ups desiring to maximize the benefits of analytics in their business.

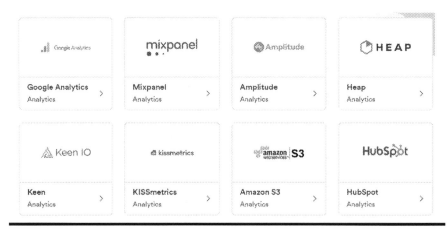

Figure 8.4 Predictive analytics in product development value chain (Adapted from Joshi and Kansupada (2020).)

Choose the Right Analytics Team

Data analytics can be complicated if the right team is not assembled. What was once the domain of Excel spreadsheet enthusiasts has now become a specialized skill for data analysts and scientists. While Excel still has its place, entrepreneurs will be able to get a lot more out of data if they hire a team with more advanced skills. A good data analytics team *will* need spreadsheet skills, but analysts should also have data analytics programming skills in Python, R or SQL, as well as a good grasp of statistics. They need to know what is realistic for start-up. A data scientist with a doctorate and ten years of experience in deep learning for autonomous driving might look great on paper, but he may not have the level of industry experience needed by a start-up. Keep high, but reasonable, expectations when hiring data analysts, and look for talented individuals with room to grow as your start-up grows.

Collect the Right Data

Data is the foundation of your data analytics. Even the best analysts in the world will not be able to do much for if they do not have good data to work with. Start-up must be sure they have the data they need for accurate and meaningful analysis. If they are in doubt of what they need, they should consult their analysts. If they have the right team, they will have a clear idea of what is needed and what is not. For example, a start-up in ecommerce will almost certainly have Google Analytics or some other analytics tool set up already. However, they may also want an extension or package to handle A/B testing to see how different page layouts or copy affects user experience. As an ecommerce company, would you need a heatmap to see how click patterns work?

Probably not. However, a start-up that is building a mobile game would love this type of insight, and could use it to improve the product by making specific interface choices informed by player actions. What a start-up will need depends on the specifics of the business. Deciding what data to collect is an aspect he should research into and implement as early as possible, because the better the data quality, the more effective the analysts can be in their analysis and the better the intended output.

Make Key Technology Decisions Early

Similarly, it is important that start-ups choose their tech stack early. A company that is built on a faulty foundation is not likely to thrive, and constantly switching out the solutions in its stack will wreak havoc with your data analytics. The choices made by start-ups, including fundamental technological ones like databases, will affect the types of analyses they can perform. A poor choice of infrastructure can be debilitating. *NoSQL* databases like *MongoDB* have become popular in recent years as they allow for quick scaling and building of product. However, this comes at the cost of being able to perform joins across data types. Traditional SQL databases like *MySQL* and *PostgreSQL* are much better at this. While it may not seem like start-ups need those features at their infancy, they must keep in mind that any changes to their system once it is up and running are likely to be disruptive and expensive. Therefore, it is better to start out with a tech stack and a database solution they can grow into, which will not limit the types of analyses their team can perform.

Measure Your Results

Start-ups should establish key performance indicators for their data analytics team. They must measure the return on investment in data analytics based on established criteria. For instance, Facebook has an analytics team which measures how relevant a post is to a user and its success is tied to this measurement. Being able to measure data team's effectiveness is key. However, moderation is key to avoid going overboard. A common mistake is having too many metrics. The data analytics team must then balance multiple measurements, and it will be difficult to narrow focus. Like any other team, the data team needs a clear direction, so pick one or two KPIs and stick with them.

Find the Supportive Investors

The right investors can be the make-or-break factor in data analytics for a start-up. Some investors may scoff at the idea of a team solely devoted to data analytics, thinking it is only needed at a larger scale. Other investors will demand an experienced analyst as an early hire before they experience data surge. Ideally, entrepreneurs want to find investors who understand that a start-up should have a data analytics team when data is available to assess. The older the data gets, the less useful insight it can provide, so once an entrepreneur is at the point of generating and collecting data, it makes sense to bring in an analyst or analytics team to help monetize it.

Growth Hacking for Start-ups

One of the biggest uses for data analytics at a start-up is growth hacking. Often, it is valuable to know what kinds of things correlate with users signing up for your site, or making a purchase so that one can double-down on strategies that prompt users to do those things. For example, early on in its development, file hosting provider Dropbox analysed its data and concluded that users who shared a file on their platform were more likely to be repeat users. They never figured out exactly why because all that mattered was the result. Dropbox rearranged its website to make sharing more accessible, and added hints to prompt users to share. Their user count skyrocketed because of the changes to the platform. It was analysing the data and discovering the connection between shares and user signups that made Dropbox's growth spurt possible. There is the likelihood that entrepreneurs will want the data team to be in search of similar insights at their business. Once they are able to systematically identify the actions that lead to the customer growth, their business will surely gain competitive edge and this will invariably lead to a growth in revenue.

Conclusion

In this chapter, an attempt was made at conceptualizing NPD in contemporary times. From the preceding sections, it was observed that the newness of a new product is multidimensional. Therefore, it behoves on the firm to identity the strategy that best fits its intended objective of birthing a new product. The increasing level of technological advancement has opened more vistas to seamlessly achieve this goal. Increasingly, product developers now rely heavily on analytics to improve every stage of NPD. This chapter also discusses the importance of entrepreneurship analytics for young entrepreneurs and highlights how start-ups can maximize the huge potential of analytics to advance their business.

References

Bianchini, M. & Michalkova, V. (2019). Data analytics in SMEs: trends and policies. *Working Paper 15*. OECD SME and Entrepreneurship. https://dx.doi.org/10.1787/1de6c6a7-en.

Chen, H.H., Kang, H.-Y., Lee, A.H.I., Xing, X., & Tong, Y. (2007). Developing new products with knowledge management methods and process development management in a network, *Computers in Industry*, vol. 59, no. 2–3, 242–253.

Cooper, R.G. (2019). The drivers of success in new-product development, *Industrial Marketing Management*, vol. 76, 36–47.

Corrocher, N. & Zirulia, L. (2010). Demand and innovation in services: the case of mobile communications, *Research Policy*, vol. 39, no. 7, 945–955.

Dataquest. (2020). *Data Analytics for Startups: What You Need to Know*. Retrieved from: https://www.dataquest.io/blog/data-analytics-startups-what-you-need-to-know/.

Griffin, A. (1997). PDMA research on new product development practices: updating trends and benchmarking best practices, *Journal of Product Innovation Management*, vol. 14, 429–458.

Johne, F.A. & Snelson, P.A. (1988). The role of marketing specialists in product development, *Proceedings of the 21st Annual Conference of the Marketing Education Group*, Huddersfield, vol. 3, 176–191.

Joshi, A. & Kansupada, H. (2020). *Predictive Analytics: Accelerating & Enriching Product Development*. Cognizant, pp. 1–8.

Loch, C.H. & Kavadias, S. (2008). Managing new product development: An evolutionary framework. In C.H. Loch & S. Kavadias (Eds.). *Handbook of New Product Development Management*. (pp. 1–666). Oxford, UK: Elsevier.

Schumpeter, J.A. (1934). *The Theory of Economic Development: An Inquiry into Profits, Capital, Credit, Interest, and the Business Cycle*. New Brunswick, NJ: Transaction Publishers.

Trott, P. (2017). *Innovation Management and New Product Development*. Edinburgh, UK: Pearson Education.

Chapter 9

Predictive Learning Analytics in Higher Education

Lawal O. Yesufu

Higher Colleges of Technology

Contents

Section 1: Introduction

Over the past decade, the explosion of smart technology, artificial intelligence (AI) and algorithm machine learning have added a new dynamic to every layer of higher education institutions (HEI) around the world. Naturally, HEI are a fertile ground for fresh ideas and innovative growth and are thereby dramatically impacted by this proliferation of efficient, calculated, pattern-recognition software. Like traditional businesses, HEI have customers, students and other stakeholders to consider while prioritizing the education of students first. Balancing the optimal well-being of students with the costs of such endeavours becomes a challenging balancing act that places pressure and stress on HEI and their members of faculty.

Just like universities adopted the email infrastructure about 30 years ago and campus-wide wireless internet infrastructure about 20 years ago, the 'smart technology' revolution of the past ten years has brought predictive analytics to the forefront and fabric of higher education management. While critics have plenty of valid points to argue about the early stages of these malleable neural networks, it is clear that if done correctly, these new AI intelligence systems and applications can stabilize university financial and organizational structures while also providing students with a guiding, responsive hand to walk them along their college path. Such a helping hand, while simple in its efficacy, can boost university retention and graduation rates by over 30% (Colvin et al., 2016).

It is important that we place the value and purpose of predictive analytics in the proper societal perspective. In the 21st century, this separation of millions of students from a formal degree through high dropout rates has further pushed students' debts into historically highs. Concerned by this deepening financial trend and the socioeconomic inequality that results from inequitable education, federal and regional governments have begun withholding money from HEI with falling graduation rates. At this point, many smaller universities are struggling to, as they say, 'pay the bills' and tens of universities risk closing within the next decade. It seems undignified to describe the funding for a university as 'paying the bills', especially when they hold the sacred duty of preparing a generation of citizen-scholars and intelligent workers for their future. However, this is evident of how dire the budget concerns currently are for state and public university systems. Thus, college and university management are willing to turn to possible solutions – including the data-driven practice of predictive learning analytics.

In the context of higher learning environments, predictive analytics refers to machine learning and AI programs that utilize large datasets, such as student gradings and attendance patterns, demographics, income brackets, Wi-Fi activity, academic progression, to create powerful algorithms for analysing such datasets in order to help universities to predict future student outcomes. Such networks would give universities a chance to intervene and make better-informed decisions based on all the information synthesized from their data gathering efforts, e.g. polls, surveys, grading reports and online activities. In this sense, predictive analytics could further personalize each student's learning experience by providing a 'one-size-adapts-to-all' revolutionary faculty-student paradigm.

In this chapter, we will review the fundamental applications of predictive analytics in higher education management, the arguments for and against its implementation, develop an ethical framework to model, guide and govern these machine-driven systems and use specific case studies to examine the positive and negative consequences of predictive analytics and how they impact on student and faculty decision-making. As the 21st century accelerates into a data-sharing blur, and as AI machinery moves exponentially faster, it could easily prove omnisciently adept at highlighting important, perhaps problematic, patterns in higher education management that could then be honestly and humbly addressed. Such a future could be as little as 10 years away.

While we will use clear examples to show how predictive analytics could fail students and faculty implications, the author acknowledges a pure, undeniable reality: AI in higher education is an inevitability, not a debate. The debate to consider is the proper application and clear high-level decisions that need to be made in consultation with all moving parts in higher education. Implemented with patience and collaboration, predictive analytics could connect universities around the world and push our understanding of pedagogical theories to new heights. We must balance this excitement with the misconceptions pattern-recognition software could lead us to.

A further point to be understood here is that predictive analytics is not intended to replace or consolidate university faculty and management. Rather, the ideal use of it would be to work synergistically with faculty by freeing them up from tedious tasks such as approving and reading through thousands of applications, basic classification of different student bodies and other time-consuming ventures that take away faculty from being a constant and direct line to student needs. In other words, it could cut university costs while simultaneously enriching its resources and information. How could anyone argue with leaning of unnecessary expenses and activities, while simultaneously adding more help for counsellors? These individualized, highly detailed student reports delivered on a massive scale represent the inherent potential of predictive learning analytics (PLA).

Section 2: Prospects and Challenges of Predictive Analytics

One may ask at this point, why predictive analytics, driven by AI and machine learning, is stirring up so such debate among HEI, the business community and private sector. As with any transformational technology, there are incredibly alluring aspects and serious dangers that threaten the proper implementation of such a powerful device or tool in our university systems.

Prospects

In this section, we will review the beneficial prospects and undeniable challenges facing predictive analytics mainstream integration into university systems faculty protocol. Proponents of the technology argue these expert neural networks will save the university system by achieving the following three goals:

1. *Cut administrative costs and enrich student financial support*:
   The first major prospect of PLA is a basic, yet ideal, scenario for any institution – lowering overhead expenses while boosting resources, assets and student datasets. The fact that machine-driven expert networks can achieve both at once immediately sets it apart from all other initiatives. HEI might exhaust trying to better reach and engage their respective student body. Such outreach is crucial, in the United States for instance, since late 2000s federal aid to HEI has been increasingly tied to student graduation and retention rates (Dahlvig et al., 2020). As a result, many colleges have struggled to find ways to substantially increase these performance indicators without over-extending their budget.

   The implementation of PLA would allow higher education board members and faculty to reorganize their student advertising and outreach programs – to both current students and prospective ones around the country. After the initial investment in a reputable PLA technology, university counsellors would be freed up to provide more one-on-one and personalized guidance to students because machine learning programs take over some of the logistical 'heavy lifting' and thus help inform the counsellors about each student's pattern of success, failure and need. Counsellors and academic advisors are therefore able to pour all their energy into flexing their 'soft skills' of encouragement, engagement and memorable interaction with the students they help on a week-to-week basis. These advisors and faculty members would be able to access interesting bits of information about any of the students they help at the click of a mouse while navigating a fully integrated database. For example, a counsellor could be alerted that a biology major is showing early trouble in a crucial math course and should immediately sign up for math tutoring with the source provided. This simple yet effective intervention can save the college careers of thousands of students.

2. *Have customized insightfully detailed student information*:
   In addition to cutting costs, the payoff of AI-driven PLA comes in the incredible bank of information it provides for the counsellors by centralizing their understanding of each student through a customized dashboard which displays the most important 'milestone markers' for a particular student in their hand-picked major. Higher education management teams have never had the opportunity to access so many different angles of collecting, organizing and interpreting bits of data. A primary application of this milestone

marker concept comes in the form of an early warning alert system (EWS). Continuing to centre the conversation on the overall prospect of this targeted, precise insight that pattern-recognition software can bring to HEI, it will be able to spot warning signs months to years before a college counsellor would have the work time to sift through so much pattern-heavy, seemingly meaningless bits of collated data.

3. *Revolutionize e-learning through real-time updated adaptive learning software*: While we will get more into e-learning later in this chapter, we wanted to touch upon the topic here as well – AI technology is naturally a strong partner of internet-based learning models. With the world moving more and more toward efficient and real-time remote technologies, adaptive learning will become a buzzword representing a dynamic software that changes, question to question, its approach to each student based on the amount of time, tries and work they enter into the system. This whole new level of interactive responsiveness will complement teaching by essentially providing a 'home virtual AI bot tutor' to every student who accesses the university Wi-Fi. Such an improvement has been tested around the world, and results, while mixed, certainly merit more investment in machine learning virtual homework programs.

Challenges

However, while saving money, giving students a stronger helping hand and optimizing an online learning environment all sound wonderful in the 21st century, technologies as powerful as AI and machine learning also have their dangers and drawbacks. Outspoken critics come from all parties involved: teachers, students, parents, university faculty and university donors and stakeholders. While many can conceptually grasp the hypothetical benefits of smart technologies complementing existing higher education infrastructure, they worry that the negatives simply outweigh the positives – that machine learning weaving into a university's function and decision-making will lead to worse, more disparate and outright disappointing results and consequences. Detractors of predictive analytics in higher education management generally bring up a few points of contention:

1. *AI software will have built-in human biases causing further inequality*: While machine-based learning has its benefactors, some management teams have argued it will only reproduce biased outcomes that reflect the creators of the AI, machine learning admissions and higher education software (Marcinkowski et al., 2020). This structuralist perspective points out that college biases have existed within human admission and enrolment decisions at universities for years – why else would a federal programme like 'affirmative action' attract so much attention?

When AI software is built for any university, critics might fear that the biases of the software creators and faculty will just carry over to the program itself, further cementing systemic forms of discrimination at HEI. Reproducing these ill-considered societal biases at an infrastructural level is very dangerous – it allows data to become highly manipulated and presented without the client's, higher education stakeholders', full knowledge of what the system does with the data.

A common concern espoused is that an AI program would discourage outreach to low-income students because they, according to the software, have low graduation and retention rates anyway. However, a computer program fails to understand the societal context that puts the student in that at-risk position; it just reads numbers off a board and makes suggestions for optimizing key performance factors. Nowhere in that description, however, is it accounting for helping at-risk students overcome the real-life, situational obstacles standing in the way of their college degree. Thus, there is a possibility of using AI-crunched data to make intellectually dishonest arguments about a student's prospective success or failure.

2. *Invasion of privacy, leading to selling of data and massive breaches*:
   Instead of using the system to conduct early reach-out and helpful intervention, some fear that universities will use it to streamline their admissions process and weed out poor students rather than helping them succeed against the odds. There is a risk that such figure-heavy, data-driven analysis threatens to turn universities into entities that function like a for-profit business with stakeholders reporting quarterly earnings. Such attitudes work in a Wall Street environment but are sickeningly shameful to bring to an educational institution. Not only that, such profiteering attitudes would simply fail to help the university build a strong alumni network. It's just a good reminder that HEI fundamentally receive and build funding differently from a publicly trading company, so they should not be encouraged to masquerade like one after adopting a PLA expert network.

Critics fear that universities will not give a real data opt-in clause to students, and will instead secretly collect mountains of data on their habits, selling it to partnered ed-tech/social media companies. Others remind us that massive companies like Yahoo and Equifax experienced data breaches that potentially destroyed the privacy of thousands. What is stopping a hacking network from accessing a humble university system and collecting each student's social security number? How can colleges safeguard and assure students such an outcome could never happen? Could they put 'Fort Knox'-level protections in front of personally vital information? These are the questions that continue to be debated regarding the issue of privacy in predictive analytics at HEI. Many do not want a dystopian future where an AI bot follows you around, notifying you when you have a survey to fill out 'for the interests of the university database'. Management teams should work to avoid PLA feeling intrusive and off-putting to students (Colvin et al., 2016).

However, students need to understand why some faculty offices would feel the need to overstep the line in an effort to collect accurate information: those collected datasets inform the algorithm created by IT, and if the data collection is poor, then the PLA prediction software will, naturally, reflect this poor data quality with even poorer college advising and enrolment suggestions. If the data collated by institutions is incomplete, incorrect or contains other factual errors, it will provide poor insight that could negatively impact entire graduating classes of students. What makes gathering these figures difficult? Data must be both expansive and specific – a challenge for universities trying to build large machine learning and data-collection infrastructures. In other words, the data collected must help inform the decision-making in highly specific, individualized student cases by comparing it to universalized, 'uniformly imputed' institutional data. Balancing these two interests can fray decision-making and further confuse both students and faculty.

Section 3: Ethical Framework and Considerations for Predictive Analytics in Higher Education

As touched on in the previous section, the potential of predictive analytics in HEI is both great and terrible in equal measure. Used the right way, it could save the existence of hundreds of colleges across the countries, such as the United States, while also achieving the graduation of students at record rates. Used improperly, it could lead to a newsworthy national controversy that would shatter the institution from student lawsuits and lead to withholding of public and private funding.

To avoid the latter outcome, a proper application of such powerful AI machine software becomes the primary issue. Like with any delicate-yet-powerful practice, a strong ethical framework must be in place for the application of PLA. Its codified values must routinely be considered to ensure higher education's employment of predictive analytics stays pure to the student body and faculty. In this section, we will outline how universities can construct honest and ethical frameworks that encourage, reassure and benefit students impacted by predictive analytics.

After reviewing the four primary ethical questions that frame the place of predictive analytics in higher education, some specific ethical-focused actions that all faculty would have to commit to for making the hypothetical of predictive analytics a mainstream reality are the following.

> Ethical Questions #1: Which staff groups/members have access to what bits of student data?

While PLA is primarily still in its 'trial' phase, higher education management should hold weekly meetings to observe and analyse what decisions the AI bot is making, and based on the collation of what data points? To be truly effective, groups of software engineers and college counsellor faculty must work together to constantly update, tweak and even completely alter the algorithms guiding the expert network's data-pattern-recognition software.

Why are these constant meetings so deeply encouraged? Because the group most affected by the big decisions these machines will make are the students, and any student body must feel the highest degree of confidence in the fairness and quality of the decisions the AI software makes. To make sure tensions and frustrations don't boil over to a university-wide/public scale, a human liaison team must constantly ask for feedback from the students in a way that caters to their concerns, perceptions and criticisms. This willingness to admittedly make errors and immediately correct any mistakes the AI makes are crucial in the early stages of implementing predictive analytics at the management level. If these thoughtful steps are not taken by faculty, a university could suffer massive and even irreparable reputational damage if predictive analytics come to be unfair, intrusive and unnecessary by the student body. To bring the best outcomes for both university management and students alike, one should consider and reflect on all dimensions, levels and spectrum that come with AI-powered, big data-driven predictive analytics.

Deciding if academic counsellors can share student Wi-Fi activity with professors and whether professors can share attendance records would be examples of making sure data does not fall into the wrong hands. Information should not be universally shared by all staff members; limits should be placed based on that team member's acting capacity and responsibility.

> Ethical Question #2: What will higher education management faculty
> be using these brackets and terabytes of data for?

It is important that colleges and universities devise legal contracts that students can plainly read exactly to what ends their data was collected for. For example, some colleges may be in a partnership with a publisher or online learning platform – do these companies get access to personal student data? If so, HEI need to divulge such information.

If higher education management has clearly defined obvious and pressing rationale for employing PLA modelling at their schools, most ethical issues of using student data can be avoided. Let's say universities want to understand why so many biology majors fail at the same semester in the second year – is there some pattern to their undergraduate pathway that improperly prepares biology majors? Is there some prerequisite course that gives insight into whether biology majors can avoid wasting two years in a major they, with a high probability, will end up dropping?

This given example is such a school-specific problem for which PLA can certainly become a huge tool. It is simply important for higher education management teams to remember AI academic software is not a data-mining enterprise; it is a 'surgically-targeted' approach that picks out cognitive patterns and academic milestone markers no human could possibly replicate at scale. Should a school improperly sell or misuse student data, however, it could easily become grounds for the school's immediate closure. That is how serious the 'data-sharing' issue can be for higher education management.

Ethical Questions #3: How will data be collected by universities, and how will students be informed of what the data will be used for – is an 'opt-in clause' clearly and plainly provided?

It is also important that whenever universities find an opportunity to harvest data, they make it plain, in very clear terms, that the activity in question will send feedback to a centralized AI-learning server. That way, students have a chance to 'opt-in' or 'opt-out' of their personal data being tracked. Let's say, for example, the university is trying to help students with late-night classes to optimize their schedule. They ask the students to disclose when they work out at the university recreation centre, and inform the student they will start collecting data and the time and place of each 'clock-in' to the recreation centre – for the purpose of generating AI recommendations about when late-night students would best experience a workout during the day before class. However, some students might feel that the information about when they exercise is intrusive and makes them self-conscious about their physical activity level. In these instances, the university needs to provide an 'opt-out' clause for that data collection method.

The same goes for any survey or poll or questionnaire provided by the school – it is the morally responsible action to provide a real 'opt-out' clause that does not trick or deceive the student body. If they say 'no', that data point is not saved or collected on any server. A breach of this student-institutional trust could, again, be grounds for the school's closure due to misuse and manipulation of such a powerful technology.

Ethical Question #4: How will bias be monitored? How will higher education management convene to make final decisions over what the AI recommends?

Finally, university faculty must work to ensure data is not used to push students away or ignore underserved, statistically unimpressive communities, economically and academically speaking. Again, routine meetings and constant evaluation of results must be a requirement for all management parties who have access to the troves of student data being collected. When they meet, boundaries must be set so everyone feels they are in an open space where serious concerns can be aptly raised and freely discussed amongst the staff. Software engineers and university faculty (admission, guidance counsellors, provosts, board members) need to create a teamwork-centred environment brimming with fully collaborative communication within the different offices.

Most importantly, faculty must also meet separately to do a thorough review of what decisions the data-driven AI software is recommending in real time. Faculty should closely compare the patterns the machine is catching in student information to the reality and experience the faculty are observing on the ground, so to speak. Racial, minority and class bias must be analysed, and the demographics of incoming classes should be compared to the makeup of past years to ensure the computer is not reproducing systemic discrimination among HEI.

Section 4: The Application of Predictive Analytics in Higher Education

After considering the ethical considerations that arise from implementing PLA models on campus, higher education management teams would benefit from knowing the five major categories that machine learning software has successfully complemented and aided faculty goals. Below, we will review each category in depth, providing various perspectives and an overall comprehension of PLA's current application within a higher education infrastructure.

Student Academic Advising

Student academic advising is unique in that it enables the provision of major guidance, potentially changing, for better or worse, the life of students forever. Unlike university staff that deal with enrolment, academic advising needs insight that tells the counsellor what major path suits each individual student best, and what path the student should take based on their past, present and forecasted future performance. With the application of PLA to academic advising offices, higher education faculty will collaborate closely with IT departments to learn their institution's specific student data insight dashboard. They will need to learn how to do various searches/queries and comparisons of students in current majors to graduates of the past; how to navigate the AI data server itself; how to craft visual graphics that represent the data's significance; and how to determine correlational relationships between the various academic, social and economic variables that influence a student's life and performance.

While academic advisors have cemented their status as a necessary appendage of the higher education system, there is usually a constant tension since advisors are understaffed and assigned to too many students. At schools with these kinds of issues of tight budgetary in the academic advising offices, PLA can play a key role in filling any gaps the human advisors miss when making major recommendations to students. A great example is given here of just how insightful AI could be in aiding faculty advise students to an incredible career path: imagine a counsellor recommends a general biology major changes to molecular biology due to high achievement (98%) in a 'History of Infectious Diseases' course that predicts major success (99% graduation rate) in molecular biology major, but only when the student scores above 95 in the 'predictor' class. The general biology major, already interested in science, would be shocked to find out that his or her grade in a history class would be such a major predictor of success in molecular biology – and that is the point and power of PLA at universities. Such interesting trends that seem like non-sequiturs when taken one at a time help counsellors make decisions based on not isolated data from one student, but how that one student is comparing to the past ten classes that graduated with a molecular biology degree. In that massive scope of analysis, the academic advising counsellor can make suggestions that will seem prescient a year or two later.

To make these kinds of excellent and unique academic suggestions, however, advisors will need close training and collaboration with IT departments to learn how to navigate their institution's AI dashboard. The AI server faculty will have access to what has been described by some as a kind of 'data mart' that allows advisors to take in the full breadth of their school's past and present graduates. From there, the advisor can ask if the student is ok having their personal academic data, demographics, grade reports, attendance, online activity, campus engagement, major choice, etc., and compared to past and current students. If the student decides the option will truly help solve the issue, they come in to be advised about, then they can 'opt-in' and have their data pulled up on the advisor's dashboard. Advisors will then need training to understand how to identify the different milestone markers that illuminate each major path.

After analysing a student's academic and personal motivation and self-efficacy data, PLA software will also give counsellors a chance to synthesize that data with student engagement levels and reported 'use of support services'. Ironically, all these different kinds of data paint a very full picture of the student the advisors have in front of them. They can learn if the student has spent immeasurable amounts of time locked in his dorm playing video games, has been going to the gym then suddenly stopped, was in two academic clubs but then dropped the science one in favour of theatre arts or has reported feeling lonely and struggling to adapt to campus life in their freshman year. All of these pieces of insight could be the clue an advisor needs to have their 'wow' moment with a student, thereby establishing a true connection that makes the student feel like they can open up and say out loud to the advisor exactly what they want out of their college experience and life in general.

However, to demonstrate to their peers and students their deep comprehension of what they are presenting, advisors will need further formal guidance on how to analyse, prepare and present visual graphics that relate the significance of various insight provided by the PLA expert network. Again, we reiterate that a collaborative process with the IT department must be accepted by the advisors and that the process will require patience. Academic advisors need to learn the fundamentals of taking information from the data mart and student insight dashboard to make impactful, meaningful presentations and decisions based on the pooled datasets. That way, they can talk to fellow faculty and the students they work with about their ongoing academic competency, their self-efficacy, their access and use of support services, and their level of student-campus engagement.

Finally, advisors will need to understand the statistical significance and weighted relationship between the different variables that impact a students' overall academic performance. Having comfortability reflecting on how a student's demographic makeup, pre-college academic report, first-term completion statistics and socioeconomic environment impacts their performance and perspective in relation to their peers is crucial to giving each student the personal care they deserve. These variables surely interact and intersect in unexpected ways, so it is important that advisors know how to draw the true significance from these numbers and survey bubbles to create a picture that is fully formed when advising students.

Adaptive Learning

As was touched upon in Section 2, adaptive, dynamic e-learning platforms have also carved out their own place in 21st-century learning models. Especially if future pandemics and disasters keep people homebound, virtual 'adaptive learning' represents a step forward in utilizing internet resources for truly valuable, engaging learning environments that help students remember and apply each lesson they take in. Maybe one day we will all have personal robot tutors like in Will Smith's *I, Robot*, but for now we will stick to describing the next step from static to adaptable online courseware.

The biggest keys to adaptive learning are lessons in self-efficacy, and what PLA would call modified learning routes, based on a student's area of struggle or need. Let's start by making one point very clear, however – these AI pattern-recognition machines will never be able to replicate the experience and inspiration of a professor working directly with a student, giving them a true vision of what they could be in the future. That job remains sacred even in the AI age, and we should recognize and acknowledge the role mentors/teachers fulfil in our society. They help provide generations with the tools to make the world what they want, and this creation of the world AI could never fulfil the same purpose.

However, in a supplemental role to direct teaching methods, AI-based dynamic learning is going to explode into something amazing and unrecognizable ten years from now. Using predictive analytics courseware, PLA trial colleges can literally modify a student's learning route, in real time, based on a confluence of elements regarding the student's online engagement. Every bit of data about how the student answers, goes through and manages his online coursework is assessed, stored and compared to years of past student records/performance. It can help the student receive more targeted, individually tailored help at home when the teacher simply is not available, and this is the perfect time for AI – to take over the teacher during off hours. It would not be wild to say that by 2030 there will be blue chip ed-tech learning companies that make adaptive learning courseware for all levels of education, but especially higher-level institutions, where good investment in such uniquely flexible software can be made.

By moving quickly through material, students demonstrate a mastery of, and getting, extra practice in areas they are measured to take more time; students can have unlimited amounts of practice that respond directly to how the last 5, 10 or 20 questions went. In math, the unbridled potential of AI adaptive learning could help English majors master their calculus requirement, biology majors get extra reading about their humanities midterm, and chemistry majors gain more organic chemistry molecules to analyse for their big final. The idea of a dynamic learning algorithm generating new questions in direct, adjustable response to the student is a fascinating one we hope to see take off with the other fruits of PLA's labour.

Executed in an ideal environment, 'adaptive assignments' become the 'day-to-day' homework and learning material, while class discussion and individual projects reflect the summative knowledge and know-how applicative wisdom gained from interacting with the AI interface. In other words, the arenas to prove the power of knowledge gained and applied during the semester still comes from engaging with peers in the classroom and the teacher regarding individual project critiques. However, AI can begin to take over the heavy workload of thinking how to cater to each student's learning needs by analysing their past records, their current performance and a bevy of other university information. From their trove of programmable content, the AI computers can generate entirely novel problems and methods of explanation. These are tasks a good teacher can certainly perform at least at the same level (if not far superior), but the power of AI is its scalability – the teacher cannot be in every student's home every night, adjusting lesson plans in real time based on how the student is responding question-by-question. They could do it for a group of several at most, but AI gives a commendable effort in mimicking that teacher's responsiveness to every single student through a dynamic adaptive learning platform.

Mini-Case Study: Intellipath at Colorado Technical University

A small example of adaptive learning can be found at Colorado Technical University (CTU), where the university has developed its own AI-programmed software – Intellipath – to assist with semester grades, class passage rates and e-learning engagement. As is recommended for early adopters of PLA and adaptive learning techniques, CTU unveiled the pilot program in 2012 and trained 800 of its faculty members (82%) to become fluent in the particulars of Intellipath's software. CTU's early adoption of such a model is a reminder of how work-intensive setting up AI course offerings can be: it took four years to set up only 15% of the university's total course offerings through the Intellipath adaptive learning platform. However, the number of students utilizing the software immediately proves the software's incredible power and promise: in 2016, CTU had over 30,000 students taking courses on Intellipath – an incredible success that raised passage rates and grade letters by statistically significant (perhaps profound) amounts.

For business, such promise of adaptive e-learning means the next few years should see billions of dollars of investment into the education sector – primarily towards implementing adaptive learning models like Intellipath. In fact, Garter Inc. has forecast these multibillion-dollar investments will continue for the next decade, as has analysis conducted by Villanova University. After being properly set up and installed, the return on investment (ROI) on big data PLA infrastructure has exponential potential.

Management of Student Enrolment

Most universities started to use the application of predictive analytics as a recruitment and admissions effort to target larger and more accurate pools of potential high school students. It was only later that PLA evolved and branched off into student care/advising, e-learning platforms and class retention efforts. However targeted enrolment, the initial spark of PLA's motivation, has been in full effect for the past decade, piloting as early as 2008 in some institutions.

Targeted student enrolment driven by predictive analytics involves creating a statistical regression model to current prospective or enrolled students 'to determine the likelihood that they will exhibit the desired outcome (dependent variable)'; that is to apply, enrol, persist or graduate. Based on any institution's individual set of data, their recruitment models will vary according to their academic scope, purpose and need.

In practice, PLA started with universities looking to extend their base of potential students by buying basic bits of names and data from K-12 Education Boards (e.g. College Board/ACT Test Maker). Partnering with the makers of these 'college readiness' tests (ACT/PSAT/SAT), universities buy the names of individuals along with a 'package' of data that included the following information: demographics (ethnicity/zip code/personal identifying markers), academic reports (ACT score, high school transcripts, surveyed personal interests, parental education) and more valuable datapoints that would give more accurate modelling of who is truly more or less likely to apply to the university, stay and graduate.

From there, universities would target these students with advertising through email and other various electronic communication; in fact, many students now are familiar with suddenly getting seemingly random emails from out-of-state universities after excelling on the SAT/ACT test. If any of these students were confused on how that college happened to get their contact information, it came through that university buying this targeted information from the SAT/ACT database in the early stages of predictive analytics applied to higher education enrolment modelling.

As AI-driven targeted enrolment has proliferated in the past decade, a fundamental approach by universities has been to take their banks of past, current and future data to create a logistic regression model that explains the relationship between 'probability of enrolment' to all the different academic/socioeconomic/personal variables mentioned above. Based on how universities weight the significance of each variable (e.g. sophomore year grades vs. parental income and educational level) in comparison to 'probability of enrolment', the model will give different suggestions and predicted future outcomes.

A major point of caution is worth reiterating here: these statistical regression models, based on how the various independent variables are entered and weighted, can lead to horrific inequitable opportunity amongst students. This would constitute a worst-case scenario regarding the application of predictive analytics in higher education and could easily bankrupt any university if it were to be sued by a student for unfair or corrupt admission practices. The perception of being an institution which uses AI algorithms to systemically discriminate outcomes between different zip codes would deepen inequality, raise student debt and slowly hollow out the student base for universities to advertise to.

For example, if the regression model created by the university's software recommended that it stop targeting youth from the poorest neighbourhood within 500 square miles because only 50 students have attended in the past 20 years from that area, it would represent the 'pulling away of opportunity' by the university for the kids from these areas to be not worth the time, value and effort to recruit. Thus, a warning, such an attitude could create even worse outcomes if predictive analytics is applied corruptly.

On the flip side (and thankfully so), plenty of companies have successfully (and ethically) expanded university outreach and advertising through the application of predictive analytics. EAB, a major ed-tech and research company, provides a great example in how predictive analytics applied to higher education enrolment strategies can reveal incredible statistical patterns that were simply invisible to the naked eye. A company leader describes below:

> One of our clients, a university in the Northeast, was already recruiting nationally but needed to expand into additional markets to meet enrolment goals.
>
> To help them, we first evaluated the university against approximately 350 schools to identify shared trends among student characteristics, demographics, and application patterns. We then drew on a national consumer database, among other data sources, to locate students with a high probability of being interested in our client.
>
> The model we developed rank – ordered 21,900 U.S. zip codes – nearly all the U.S. zip codes that had 10 or more students available to contact. The resulting map of the ranked zip codes is below, while the area highlighted in the circle represents the focus area recommended. The highest scoring markets exhibited favourable demographic and behavioural characteristics, revealing students with a high likelihood to apply.

Ironically, a college in the Northeast found its 'student enrolment salvation' deep in the heart of Texas! How else would an enrolment team working at that college find such a seemingly arbitrary region in a state thousands of miles away and say, 'There it is – we have the highest chance of success if we put our recruitment resources towards El Paso'. Without predictive analytics revealing this deep trendline, everyone in the room would have looked around and thought, 'The boss just lost his mind!' Such a remarkably nonlinear yet effective suggestion demonstrates the resource-saving exponential power of PLA in higher education.

Student Academic Performance

After student enrolment, the creation of early warning systems (EWS) at various universities piloting PLA has proven to be a resounding, overwhelming and acutely detailed success. For management in higher education, EWS have been a godsend in identifying 'at-risk' students long before they drop out. EWS get set up in each student's particular major and financial situation. Its power lies in noticing that students are getting held back from reaching their full potential on minor 'snags' – their climb back to 'good' status with the university is being held up by a curb, not a mountain. These students need only a little figurative 'push' in the right direction and timely intervention is the art of academic advising. Having predictive analytics power EWS will become one of higher education management's greatest tools to boost student retention, GPA and graduation rate.

Many universities struggle with an ongoing issue – when is the right time to call a student in and warn them about an upcoming obstacle? When is 'too soon' in that the problem comes by later in the semester and students feel a false sense of security having visited early in the year? When is 'too late' and the student finds him or herself down in a hole they cannot effectively climb out of? EWS can take away some of the concerns from faculty that they might miss their window of opportunity to help students make it all the way to achieving a college diploma. Universities all over the world have trailed forms of EWS software, partnering with outside ed-tech companies to create precise analytics that elevate a university's standing in the world of higher education.

Here is a central problem for many of the universities trying to identify 'at-risk students' – many do not receive grade reports until the seventh or eighth week of class. By then any bad trends that have set in the first month may have already carried into the second, creating a 'red-alert' scenario that could easily lead to the student dropping out. This gap of time from grade report to grade report is what can make intervention a problem – students that are good at one grade report may reverse on the next, and vice versa. At such a young age, a lot can change over two months in the life of a 19- or 20-year-old. EWS can analyse hundreds of variables, such as demographic, academic, financial, personality or campus engagements, that could contribute to a given student's potential success or failure rate. It can estimate these odds in ways humans cannot, and while that does not mean it can make as good a final decision as a human, it can help faculty catch a student the minute they start exhibiting signs of falling through the college's safety net.

In fact, adjusting a student's major choice or college finance options with a frank conversation before the failures in classes begin to accumulate can be the saving grace for student retention rates. Some universities have developed EWS that have over 800 different milestone markers that help them catch students wading into trouble the very first class they experience difficulty or 'falling off the wagon', as they say. EWS software can catch minor financial issues before a student becomes debt-ridden, and in-trial scenarios have helped students easily get on payment plans for debts under $2,000. Simple moves like this can add up each percentage point to retention rates and, in turn, make the higher education institution in question more credible and insightful when catering to its student body.

EWS programs can catch signs of minor academic faltering before it splutters into something deeper. A simple example is when a student has not attended class for three days and has had no 'clicking activity' on his e-learning platform, even though he is technically logged in. He could be sent a quick email to check that everything is OK. Welfare and academic checks can keep the student focused on why they are at university in the first place.

If students knowingly 'opt-in' to these AI-driven programs, the inputting of this valuable information just collates data the university already collects. For example, the university already notes when and where a student swipes their ID card; how often have they visited the on campus facilities (library, counselling office, academic advising, gym, cafeteria, etc.); whether they come from a high-performing high school or a more troubled area; whether their parents provide financial support to them; whether they took out student loans in their name; whether their grades from the first to the second semester parallel the grading patterns of any past students in their major who passed or failed. All these questions can be analysed and answered with predictive analytics.

As a conclusion on the conversation on EWS, we feel a need to make a special mention of Purdue University's 'Course Signals' program as it has become the 'go to' example for successful implementation of EWS software. While its overall accuracy and efficacy remains in debate, Purdue has argued that their PLA-powered efforts have boosted overall student retention by at least 20%. Avoiding the problem of waiting too late to intervene, 'signals' at Purdue have helped counsellors make successful contact with students as early as the second week. Eighty-nine percent of the students enrolled in the program have reported a positive experience. This highly favourable reaction from the most-affected group, the student body, is an excellent point to use in the promotion of the use of EWS at HEI. While the machine learning program makes the recommendation to reach out to the students, it is the professor or advisors themselves that provide the necessary help to the students. It turns out that this is what students care about most, and having the faculty personally reach out to them alleviated any concerns they had about feeling like just a random ID number. Although 'Course Signals' did report areas for improvement, some students apparently struggled with moments when multiple faculty members and instructors reached out all at once and saying different things with different levels of urgency; overall, it has revolutionized the advising office practices at Purdue University.

Predictive Analytics for Curriculum Internationalization

In this final part of Section 4, we will cover how predictive analytics can help with the continued effort towards the creation of an 'internationalized curriculum' where data shared between HEI can make its machine learning decisions more precise (Clauss et al., 2019). For the past several decades, HEI have already begun working towards a standardized set of curriculum checks that ensure any student from one part of the world will have the skills and capability to work across the globalized world (Yesufu, 2018). However, predictive analytics can push this integrative effort amongst universities even further forward, pooling massive amounts of multi-institutional data to refine curriculum to include internationalized perspectives. With PLA, HEI can partner together, creating the world's most valuable hubs of student information and curriculum refinement strategies.

Internationalization has numerous and wide-ranging benefits for the student body. It connects the students to international cultures, opens the doors to friendships, international networking and a global perspective when honing their professional development. When working to enter international politics or a business, a student with an internationalized curriculum experience will be able to analyse the same problem through multiple cultural contexts, and usually have an adaptive and comparative thinking lens through which to assess themselves to obtain self-awareness of one's own culture.

This naturalization of diversity through the internationalization of curriculum is something that, through its pattern-generating purpose, predictive analytics can improve upon in the outcomes. Students love programs that allow them to travel abroad for semesters, and the internationalization of their curriculum brings them one step closer to the world at large.

For faculty, internationalization of curriculum means finding unique, insightful ways to compile performance data on their students, and then finding helpful ways to collaborate with other HEI in a comparative, collaborative effort. By combing through and comparing the various standards for each major that different colleges have around the world, educators can make sure that, through their pooled data, they are producing students who could work anywhere, from Prague to Thailand to Abu Dhabi to South Africa to Peru (Yesufu, 2018). While each college should maintain a focus on what makes their locale worth investing in, utilizing predictive analytics can broaden international standards.

When applying the internationalization of curriculum, faculty should focus on compiling data and statistics from their adaptive learning e-platforms, as the most data points on student comprehension will come on this machine. From there, universities can compile their own dataset that reflects a sort of standardized test that encompasses all the learning and knowledge taught within a specific field of study. Then, that higher education institution can compare its pedagogical and achievement standards to its peer universities around the world. Each university can then add internationalized perspectives and elements to its curriculum filling out the students' contextual understanding of how their acquired knowledge applies to real-world scenarios and societies/cultures.

Section 5: Case Studies of Predictive Learning Analytics in Higher Education Management

Introduction

Up to this point, most of our discussion has been hypothetical and generalized for the benefit of any higher education management team. Below, we will move forward and examine multiple case studies of real universities trailing PLA algorithms to inform their faculty and decision-making processes. While some schools' implementation demonstrates the exponentially insightful pattern-seeking power of AI, the others serve as cold reminders that this technology could quickly turn generations of students into disembodied, unknowable, helpless bits of faceless data.

To avoid such a disappointing outcome with such a promising technology, university faculty must balance PLA's power amongst upper management and concentrate its use to locally specific trends not only following student grades, but their Wi-Fi activity and class engagement, active and in-person participation, number of correspondence sent with teachers, time spent active and not idle on e-learning platforms. Thus, by not leaning on the technical efficacy too much they will not forget one of the key underpinnings of their university work: that higher education is not solely about optimizing student efficiency for the sake of maximized federally subsidized profit. It is also for figuring out why you would want to achieve such an end in the first place and finding out how one's individual character can fit into the world at large for such goals. It does a disservice to all things creative and remarkable when brainless decisions are made from an error-riddled algorithm instead of decisions based on meeting people face to face and not reading too much into the bits/trails of data they leave behind.

Predictive Analytics in Georgia State and Kennesaw State Universities

Georgia State University (GSU) and Kennesaw State University (KSU) in the United States both provide excellent examples of predictive analytics for all parts of the community. As mentioned at the beginning of this chapter, a primary motivation for many schools utilizing PLA came from their alarming low graduation and consequently high dropout rates. In Georgia, where poverty strikes minority communities with a harshly acute sense, dropout rates accelerated well over the horrific 50% average across the country. In fact, Georgia State University had a disappointing 18% graduation rate among minority men, and whites did not fare much better at 32%. Unsure of how to bridge the gap to help struggling students, GSU had only one counsellor per thousand students, Georgia State turned to a 21st century salvation: predictive analytics and modelling (Dimeo, 2017).

Taking a very incisive, targeted approach to their 52,000-student body, Georgia State compiled ten years of student data to identify 800 different milestone markers that, depending on a student's particular degree ambitions, gave insight into whether they were on track GPA and credit-wise to graduate within six years. Thus, if a student ended up picking a major that their grading pattern history did not support, the algorithm could spot the potential danger before any human counsellor would have noticed – saving students red-alert issues and from going deeper into a major they are slowly unravelling in. Georgia State is referenced often in discussing PLA's application because of its incredible success; over 200,000 interpersonal, one-on-one advisor interventions were prompted by Georgia's Graduation and Progression

Success 'early warning system', and these quality student-advisor interventions have boosted Georgia State's graduation rate by 67%. Even better, researchers have noted that 'Achievement gaps between high-risk student populations and the total student body have disappeared'. In other words, PLA has been a massive, unequivocal success at Georgia State, taking all the gain PLA has to offer while avoiding its very real and deep pitfalls. Dr Tim Renick, vice president for enrolment at GSU, lauds the analytical insights PLA brings to helping students with minor financial troubles (e.g. paying $1,000 of leftover debt on semester tuition) and frequently checking in on any students that seem to be 'falling through the cracks'. Any higher education management team would want to check with GSU's 18-member board to get better insight in just how they balanced the implementation of predictive analytics, and how they turned the venture into such a resounding achievement (Dimeo, 2017).

A sister Georgia school, Kennesaw State University (KSU) achieved spectacular results with PLA-driven management interventions. KSU reduced its course failure rates by nearly half after collaborating with Perceivant, an ed-tech and digital publishing company. Like GSU, KSU faculty were deeply troubled by the number of students that signed up for their classes, only to realize that they may have gotten in over their heads. With low and fail grade rate of 50%, one can imagine how discouraging it would be for students and professors alike to watch half of each class just drop off the face of the map. Many PLA programs, KSU's included, also shine a spotlight on freshman year students – as KSU chairman Dr Kandice Porter acknowledges, 'New students really don't have all the skill sets that they need to be successful that first year of college' we realized that that students weren't spending enough time engaging with the content. PLA pointed out a simple trend to KSU staff: 'A' grade students were spending 2.5 hours per unit, while 'C' grade students were spending 20 minutes. At that point, a counsellor can simply intervene and say something to the student along the lines of the following sample counsellor-student correspondence:

> Hi there! Just wanted to point out to you that you were only logged into your math program for 15 minutes the whole week, but there is a major midterm for your class coming up! We saw that attendance was spotty last week, but we still want to ask, is everything ok? We just want to check in on you.
>
> Our odds tell us you have entered some dangerous territory of failing your class, which none of us want. Any chance we can extend a hand to schedule tutoring or some of other one-on-one work with you? Reach out to us, we're here to help you stay on to get your degree!

That simple 'extending the hand' gesture was only made possible on a large scale by PLA. With tens of thousands of students, having a system that can sift through the 'hours logged into class website' can turn from a bit of data that is meaningless at large scale for a human, but perfect for a machine to analyse and deduce helpful conclusions. These kinds of case studies provide a strong argument for the implementation of PLA. As a higher education counsellor, the ability to go through each student assigned to you and note their basic engagement markers, time online, class attendance across every year, particular class weaknesses, progress towards major requirements could conceivably become the most helpful tool in a university faculty's arsenal (Paul & MacDonald, 2020).

Predictive Analytics at Mount St Mary's University

However, not every predictive analytics case study gave promising, inspiring results like GSU and KSU. These schools struck out because of how they used advanced technology to close achievement gaps, not to systemically force students into acting out of their own best interests/autonomy. The fear, or worst-case scenario, of course, is when there can be a calculated hedge fund-type financial manager, who comes to a university's board with dreams of good numbers, rising profits and faceless students.

An investigation into Simon Newman, former Mount St Mary's University President, provides a clear and cautionary tale of how arrogant and reckless PLA can make higher education management teams – it becomes easier to disregard the well-being of students when you are solely looking at admissions and enrolment as some sort of 'quarterly report' you are submitting to company stakeholders. Newman, a former CEO of Cornerstone Management Group, represented how data analytics can bring out the worst in higher education management if not properly executed (Newman, 2016).

Newman set a reckless tone right from the start by claiming he wanted to put the higher education institution on an 'aggressive growth trajectory' – an odd, concerning and contextually inappropriate phrase to use when describing a place that moulds the future generations of America. Newman's first concern should have been the students themselves, but he instead obsessed over forcing a certain quota of students to drop out before he reported St Mary's 'first-year retention numbers' to the federal government for financial grants. He told faculty they have to let go of nurturing students like 'bunnies' and instead should imagine themselves putting a 'glock' to the heads of students who are dropping out. He then fired two professors who refused to go to the extreme lengths of excluding academically at-risk students for the sole sake of improved government figures. Newman would pontificate about bringing the 200-year old Catholic American institution into the 21st century by meeting the needs of a 'demanding global economy' with new 'technical skills' added to the liberal arts college's curriculum. Such ignorantly cut-throat, pseudo-violent, hyper-competitive 'hackery' works in the business world, but in a realm of wholesome education such comments are offensive and completely out of line – a textbook fireable offense.

The worst part of Newman's words and actions was not the fact he wanted to have frank discussions with potentially troubled students. The worst part is he did this purely for the sake of a 'student retention' stat that would be submitted to the government, crushing the very heart of any higher education. Before ever meeting any of the kids or even getting settled into the school, this man was ready to manipulate survey data to force kids out and send them packing wherever – the point is he didn't care what happened after they dropped. The numbers would have already been submitted on St Mary's University government report. The lack of consideration for student well-being in this case study is so sickening it almost merits abandoning PLA altogether. If predictive analytics were not such a time and money-saving tool for well-intentioned, underserved schools, this severe negative effect would outweigh any mild positive effect. Make no mistake – Newman's dereliction of duty and callous profiteering is a worst-case scenario of student data being used to treat kids as dolls on a string, forcing their hand by claiming you have knowledge of their 'academic forecast through AI-generated algorithm projections'. Give the students a break, they weren't born yesterday. Newman's brash petulance and manipulation of informative data demonstrates the dangers and limitations to PLA applied to higher education management.

Conclusively, considering the benefits, disadvantages, risks, ethical and applied issues relating to predictive analytics in higher education management, the ability to use historic data to predict students' performances, plan students' academic progression, increase the value of learning in context and content all indicate the immense value predictive analytics brings to higher education. However, the adoption of these AI and machine learning technologies do not replace the role of faculty and management in higher education. They do streamline and enable faculty and administrators to focus more on the human side of educational development and save them from distractions caused by the overload of manual work and the inability of people to use big data without these technologies. Predictive analytics is the future of academic development, financial management and the creation of knowledge in higher education all over the world.

References

Clauss, A., Lenk, F., & Schoop, E. (2019, October). Enhancing international virtual collaborative learning with social learning analytics. In *2019 2nd International Conference on New Trends in Computing Sciences (ICTCS)* (pp. 1–6). IEEE.

Colvin, C., Rogers, T., Wade, A., Dawson, S., Gasevic, D., Buckingham Shum, S., ... & Corrin, L. (2016). Student retention and learning analytics: A snapshot of Australian practices and a framework for advancement.

Dahlvig, C. A., Dahlvig, J. E., & Chatriand, C. M. (2020). Institutional expenditures and student graduation and retention. *Christian Higher Education*, 1–13. doi:10.1080/15363759.2020.1712561.

Dimeo, J. (2017, July 19). Data dive. *Inside Higher Ed*. https://www.insidehighered.com/digital-learning/article/2017/07/19/georgia-state-improves-student-outcomes-data.

Marcinkowski, F., Kieslich, K., Starke, C., & Lünich, M. (2020, January). Implications of AI (un-) fairness in higher education admissions: The effects of perceived AI (un-) fairness on exit, voice and organizational reputation. In *Proceedings of the 2020 Conference on Fairness, Accountability, and Transparency* (pp. 122–130).

Newman, S. (2016). Mount St. Mary's University president defends his efforts to retain students. *Washington Post*. Retrieved from https://www.washingtonpost.com/news/grade-point/wp/2016/01/20/mount-st-marys-university-president-defends-his-efforts-to-retain-students/

Paul, J. A., & MacDonald, L. (2020). Analytics curriculum for undergraduate and graduate students. *Decision Sciences Journal of Innovative Education, 18*(1), 22–58.

Yesufu, L. O. (2018). Motives and measures of higher education Internationalisation: A case study of a Canadian University. *International Journal of Higher Education, 7*(2), 155–168. doi:10.5430/ijhe.v7n2p155.

Index

Note: *Italic* page numbers refer to figures.

Printed in the United States
by Baker & Taylor Publisher Services